mixmag

DESTINATION DANCEFLOOR

**A GLOBAL ATLAS OF DANCE MUSIC AND CLUB CULTURE –
FROM LONDON TO TOKYO, CHICAGO TO BERLIN AND BEYOND**

DESTINATION DANCEFLOOR

**A GLOBAL ATLAS OF DANCE MUSIC AND CLUB CULTURE –
FROM LONDON TO TOKYO, CHICAGO TO BERLIN AND BEYOND**

mixmag

CONTENTS

AUTHOR'S NOTE

Most of the cities featured in *Destination Dancefloor* could fill an entire library with an exhaustive look at their club culture. This book is an impressionistic snapshot of their scene at the time it was written, and many incredible clubs, artists, DJs and parties have been left off the guestlist simply due to space. Keep up the good work, no slight is intended.

I just hope it gives the reader a sense of the commonalities and contrasts between the ways that every city parties, and maybe inspires you to visit and explore them for yourself. Or, just as importantly, inspires you to look around your own town or city and think about how you can create something that fuels your local club culture. Even the world's biggest, best and most famous nights started with a group of friends, a passion and an idea.

Many thanks to my co-contributors Tracy Kawalik, Shirley Ahura, Olivia Wycech, Andrew Kemp, Nicolas Dembicki, Fede Rochon, Nicolas Gonzalez, Ivi Brasil and Eduardo Oliviera, and to the many incredible people who so generously gave up their time and insight to provide the inside track on their hometown.

The roll of honour is at the end of the book – any errors, omissions or sweeping generalisations are, of course, the author's own.

See you down the front,
Duncan

FORE WORD

Clubs are at the heart of our culture, bringing together people of all backgrounds who share a common desire to be part of something special. I've spent my working life in clubs all over the world and met wonderful people and built life-long friendships.

Clubbing wasn't always the global industry it is today. There were, of course, great clubs way before the time we now call 'back in the day', like the Cotton Club in Harlem where you could dance to the likes of Louis Armstrong and Cab Calloway. You had the clubs of the '60s and '70s, before the disco explosion of the late '70s and early '80s that made sure that Saturday night would never be the same again. 'Back in the day' as we know it, though, is around 1987–1989, when the Second Summer Of Love kicked off in the UK. It transformed a small Acid House movement into a scene, which then became a culture, which grew into an industry that conquered the world.

As a DJ coming up through the rave scene, I played at clubs like the Zap in Brighton and the Eclipse in Coventry, before launching Ultimate B.A.S.E. at the Velvet Rooms in what was my first Central London residency. We'd play vinyl to a few hundred people with condensation dripping off the ceiling. There was no social media then – you promoted through word of mouth and by handing out flyers.

When I think of a club, I think of a venue packed full of people having the time of their lives, dancing to DJs as nighttime moves towards daylight. Electronic music has spread across the world and become the sound of nightlife. DJs and live artists have become household names, and the clubs themselves have achieved iconic status. Everyone has their favourite, with beloved venues like Echostage, DC10, Zouk, Ministry, and fabric following on from classics like Twilo, Rex, Paradise Garage, Haçienda , Space, and Heaven.

I'm sure that everyone who picks up this book has had their own unique experience. From first timers to seasoned partygoers, we've all had a clubbing moment that will stay with us forever. We've seen pumping dancefloors, listened to every kind of music, and shared all this with friends and strangers. We've seen a whole range of emotions, from love to sadness and everything in between.

Some of us are lucky enough to stand in clubs after everyone's gone home; the music is off, and the lights are on but the night isn't over – it's then that you can really feel the magic. I remember standing in Space in Ibiza the day after the closing night of my long-running annual residency. I'd played all night to an emotionally supercharged crowd. It had been one of the most amazing

experiences of my life and suddenly, just like that, it was over. I was standing alone in the middle of the dancefloor, but I could sense the energy in the room, as if each clubber had left an atom of themselves behind. When I closed my eyes, I could see hundreds of thousands of smiling faces. Having been on countless dancefloors over the years, it's ironic that one of my most powerful clubbing memories is being alone in an empty room.

The world has changed dramatically in recent years, with a global lockdown making us realise how much we had started to take for granted. Clubs have closed down, some have re-opened, and many new clubs have been born: testament to the fact that human beings will always feel the need to socialise and dance to great music. As I write this, I'm getting ready for my new residency in Ibiza, and I can't wait to share my hybrid live sound with the next electronic generation.

I'm so proud that our little movement grew into such a phenomenal global force. And I can't wait to see you all on the dancefloor.

Oh Yes, Oh Yes!

Carl Cox

Melbourne 2022

Dancers at Basement Club, Tunis

Chapter 1

NORTH AMERICA

Los Angeles

New York

Chicago

Detroit

Chicago

New York

Detroit

éal

D

Montreal

Chicago

Toronto

Montreal

Los Angeles

ork

Los Angeles

oronto

Montreal

Los Angeles

NEW YORK

Flamboyant fashion at Glitterbox at House of Yes

Take the last exit to Brooklyn to find the centre of the Big Apple's club scene

Some of the most revered and famous nightclubs in history were founded and found fame on the island of Manhattan, from discos like The Gallery and Studio 54 in the '70s, through Paradise Garage in the '80s, and Limelight and Twilo in the '90s. But New York's centre of club gravity has moved across the East River over the last decade, with a rash of clubs, most notably the Berlin-style Output, opening in Brooklyn.

The impact of Output can't be overstated. "I was spending a lot of time in Berlin and going to Berghain a lot," says founder Nicolas Matar, "and that inspired the ethos: a music-driven venue that was purpose built around the sound system and the acoustic treatment of the room. Music-driven, no photography, no PR, not much marketing, just very underground." Or, as former resident and techno DJ Desna puts it: "Before Output, we didn't really have any clubs that were representing underground music. They really brought a scene here."

Unfortunately, after helping to transform the area and inspire a generation, the inevitable happened: the pressure of gentrification forced Output to close in 2019. But the scene it helped to create in Brooklyn endures. At its nexus are the areas of Green Point, Williamsburg and Bushwick. The latter is home to venues like Avant Gardner (a four venue complex that hosts everyone from Amelie Lens to Defected and Elrow, and where, in 2022, Carl Cox curated his 'Brooklyn Takeover'), the post-industrial Elsewhere, Brooklyn Steel, Nowadays, the flamboyant House of Yes, and the Good Room, while invite-only club Venus In Furs (locally known as Paragon) sits on Bushwick's border with the Bed-Stuy district. But crews and collectives like Teksupport, Hot 'N Spicy, Papi Juice, The Push, School Of Hard Trax, Soul Summit (a long-running Fort Greene institution), and especially house crew Sublimate, are always seeking out new industrial spaces to occupy for a night. Look out for The Bunker NY, a long-running techno series, community and record label that DJ alumni Justin Cudmore described as "like going to techno university".

Manhattan – expensive and gentrified to within an inch of its life – is home to the stylish bars of Chelsea and the slightly more affordable East Village. For classic house music and DJ legends like Tony Humphries and Danny Krivit, Le Bain is a must (you'll find it on the top floor of the Standard Hotel). Nebula, the biggest new club to open on the island for years, is bottle service focused, but with strong bookings including the likes of Jamie Jones and Eric Prydz. Look out also for nights like Battle Hymn in Chelsea's Flash Factory, and the jazzy Nublu in locations across the East Village. If you are feeling expansive, the Knockdown Center in Queens, owned by the crew behind Elsewhere, is a favourite of local house music legend Kerri Chandler.

Yaeji, a driving force in NYC's club crews and collectives

François K, one third of Body & SOUL

Yaeji
Young Kathy Lee spent parts of her adolescence in her birthplace Queens, before moving to Atlanta, where she was the only Asian American in her school, and then on to Korea and Japan, eventually returning to the US. It was in New York, however, that she found her voice, with breakthrough release 'Raingurl'. She also found her tribe here, becoming a driving force in promoting and uniting NYC's club crews and collectives, and throwing her own inclusive and community-led parties, Elancia and Curry In No Hurry, across the city.

Body & SOUL
The holy trinity of house music in NYC, Danny Krivit, Joe Claussell and François K have been hosting their B&S parties across the city for more than 25 years. Born out of Sunday afternoon b2b2b sessions at the much missed Club Vinyl, the three work almost telepathically across the span of a night to combine their influences – disco, jazz, soul, electro, global, and even new wave – into a house groove.

DFA Records
James Murphy's globally influential label was a huge factor in New York's resurgence as the epicentre of hip music in the '00s, with releases from The Rapture, The Juan MacLean and Murphy's own LCD Soundsystem. The punk funk sound they pioneered formed a bridge between the supercool skinny-jeaned indie rock of The Strokes, Interpol, and the like, and Murphy and co-founder Tim Goldsworthy's own passion for electronic music, from krautrock and Chicago house to Daft Punk (naturally), joining the dots for dancefloors across the world.

CLUBS

Elsewhere
This live and electronic venue in the Williamsburg District of New York was built in the labyrinthine shell of a former industrial furniture assembly factory. It hosts carefully programmed live shows on two indoor stages, with bookings featuring everyone from Palms Trax to DJ Harvey, Jon Hopkins to Cinthie.

House Of Yes
Founders Anya Sapozhnikova and Kae Burke conceived of House Of Yes as an alternative performance venue and creative event space. Originally based in an erstwhile squat, the current 475-capacity venue enables them to host a plethora of events spanning circus and cabaret nights and Pride parties with Little Louie Vega, as well as staging 'Ketamine: the Musical'. "People come to House Of Yes for the community, to make friends, to learn about themselves and grow and express themselves," says Sapozhnikova.

○ RECORD SHOP

Brooklyn Record Exchange
Located, conveniently, in the same complex as Elsewhere, this clean, unfussy plywood-panelled spot is a trove of second-hand vinyl of all genres (think disco, Spanish language gospel, '80s movie soundtracks). Perhaps not the place to find the latest Drumcode release, it is the perfect spot to wile away a rainy afternoon looking for bargains and oddities. Or to unload your own collection for a fair price, should a change in life circumstances make it advisable... better to have loved and lost, etc.

THE LOFT

Break it down into its constituent elements, and what is a 'club', anyway? The template is pretty simple. A room or space that's mostly dancefloor, likely set up to create an immersive environment with low lights and decorations. A sound system, of course, sufficient to flood the senses and encourage dancing. A DJ, playing records without pause, curating the music and vibe. A crowd of people who are there for a collective experience. If it didn't exist, it would be necessary to invent it. And it was indeed invented. By David Mancuso, at a party in 1970, in his loft apartment in New York City.

Writer Tim Lawrence even puts a date on it: February 14th, when Mancuso threw his invite-only Valentine's Day party under the tagline 'Love Saves the Day' (also the title of Lawrence's great book on the subject). The idea was based on the tradition of Harlem 'rent parties' – events people in the NY borough had been throwing since the 1930s – opening their doors for a small cover charge to raise money for rent. The soundtrack was always eclectic. "It annoys me when people call David the Godfather of Disco," says Mancuso's close friend, protege and NY DJ legend Colleen 'Cosmo' Murphy, who began attending in the '80s. "Because the parties predated the genre by a few years, and he always played all sorts of things like soul, R'n'B, percussive rock, and bits of African music."

A fanatic about sound quality, his set-up was built around an extremely high fidelity system consisting of Klipschorn speakers, Mark Levinson amps and eye-wateringly expensive Koetsu cartridges, and Mancuso's tinkering and evolution would never stop. He even moved away from mixing, leaving gaps between songs so as not to degrade the perfectly pitched, never-too-loud sound; gaps that would be filled by cheers and whooping. (Though it's also possible that he just couldn't bear to end a track before its time).

Mancuso also added that other club essential: a properly inebriated crowd, mainly due to the LSD-laced punch he freely gave out. Indeed, conspiracy fans take note: Mancuso's hypnotic sets, carefully selected to create a three-act transcendental journey, were built on principles he'd discussed with acid evangelist Timothy Leary, whose own experiments with LSD at Harvard were supposedly undertaken with the covert support of the CIA. Just think about that next time you're browsing Mixcloud.

Perhaps the attendees were the real key to the enduring legacy of the Loft. "David would make sure the crowd was a mix of people from all backgrounds and sexual orientations," says Cosmo. "He'd invite a lot of people from the neighbourhood, so the make-up was very Latino and African American." He inspired others: another protege, Larry Levan, would attempt to reproduce the vibe (and sound quality, with the addition of some serious bass) at his Paradise Garage, while Nicky Siano would scale things up at The Gallery. Both of them, unlike their shamanic and spiritual role model, brought the DJ front and centre for the first time. Loft regular Frankie Knuckles would open his own club, the Warehouse, in Chicago. And David Morales was another regular who'd go on to define the city's scene for decades.

But for Mancuso, a gregarious orphan who'd grown up in children's homes, the Loft was a place to build a family (he called it "(H)ohhhmmmmm"). For many of the attendees from New York's transient population of outsiders and rejects, it was one of the few places that they could call home. Mancuso invented the concept of the club as a 'safe space', arguably the very first requisite for club culture.

David Mancuso DJs at a
Loft party in London

CHICAGO

The birthplace of house music, Chicago is so deeply steeped in the genre, so bursting with legendary figures and parties, that the city and the sound are synonymous

Chicago prides itself on having parties every night of the week. Its opening hours are, by American standards, pretty generous: 3am or 5am on Saturdays, 2am or 4am the rest of the time, complete with a very lively ticketed-if-unofficial afterparty scene. Locals describe a distinct split between the North and South Side of the city in terms of music and crowds. In the predominantly Black South Side, tradition rules. Crowds are older, or at least multi-generational, the strain of house more old school, and the DJs are often names that resonate throughout the history of house music, from Derrick Carter to Roy Davis Jr. Except for a handful of venues such as the Promontory, it's not about 'clubs'. Parties can happen anywhere: bars, restaurants, civic halls, lounges, and they aren't restricted to particular neighbourhoods, either. You won't find out what's happening on listings sites. Instead, ask the locals (who are always ready to welcome newcomers who've looked beyond the somewhat racist overtones of the area being dangerous). Look out for flyers in bars or on windshields, check out local websites like the excellent 5Mag.net and do312.com, and join the myriad Facebook groups around DJs and parties (we did say the crowd was older) before you go.

In the North Side, the music tends to be more forward-looking and international, and the audiences more mixed – accepted wisdom is that while Southsiders will venture north, Northsiders rarely venture south. Here you'll find the clubs that have fuelled the renaissance of Midwest DJs over the past few years, most notably the legendary Smartbar (a launchpad for the likes of DJ Heather and Kentucky transplant The Blessed Madonna), the 27-year-old Spybar, and Primary, PRYSM and Le Nocturne.

Chicago's winters are long and miserable, but in the summer this city's scene unfurls like the petals of a tropical flower, with countless outdoor festivals, block parties and rooftop events. Look out for the Silver Room Block Party (curated by Ron Trent, and an adjunct of a South Side shop selling African-influenced jewellery, fashion and art), the Chosen Few Picnic, run by a 45-year-strong crew of DJs and attracting crowds of 40,000 to Jackson Park for the 'Woodstock of House Music', and West Fest, with regular headliners Mark Farina and Derrick Carter. Wherever you go, dress tends to be Midwestern casual, the crowds expect to be impressed and to dance, and atmospheres are welcoming rather than elitist, in the true spirit of the city's soundtrack. As *5 Mag* Editor-in-Chief and Smartbar regular DJ Czarina Mirani aka Czboogie says: "We have a real pride in our heritage. House music is in our blood. It belongs to this city, and this city belongs to house music."

Blessed Madonna performing at Smartbar, one of Chicago's oldest homes for electronic music

DJS

Derrick Carter
Moving to the city as a suburban teen, Derrick Carter found a place where "I could find other freaks, other weirdos like me." He also found his break as a DJ, hosting semi-legal loft parties and making a name for himself as one of the foremost house DJs in the city. His reputation has since taken him all over the world, though his own productions date back to 1989 and range across banging techno, chugging house and everything in between.

Heather
Brooklyn-born Chicagoan DJ Heather may have been a fixture in the city's house scene for decades, but don't call her old school. Constantly evolving and seeking out fresh sounds to put her own twist on, her residency at Smartbar and her appearances across the city and beyond (she's a frequent guest at London's fabric) represent the very best of the Chicago spirit.

O RECORD SHOP

Gramaphone
"Gramaphone is still one of the greatest record stores in the history of dance music," says former employee Derrick Carter. Looking at the other DJs who have been on the payroll, including Mark Farina, DJ Heather and DJ Sneak, as well as the regular streamed events, who would argue?

CLUBS / EVENTS

Smartbar
Opened in 1982, with the first guest DJ to play in the club being Frankie Knuckles, Smartbar has survived through fat and lean years for electronic music in the Midwest to become one of the most important clubs in the world. Its global fame was helped by the rise of The Blessed Madonna, the club's first talent buyer and later its Creative Director. Residencies like Derrick Carter's Queen! and DJ Heather's Lake Effect are supplemented by international guests that range from Berlin's Cinthie to Japan's DJ Nobu.

Six06 Cafe
Owned by two brothers who live, breathe and DJ house music, this new venue is a Greek café-cum-club-cum-art space that's reimagining how venues work in the city by emphasizing the daytime community and the links between music, art and even food. Rooftop parties in the Summer featuring the likes of DJ Heather, Czboogie, and Ron Carroll are the highlight, along with the meze.

My House Music Festival
Created by scene catalyst and DJ M-Dok, My House is one of the few festival events that looks to contextualise the city's heritage for a young and enthusiastic crowd by putting new acts alongside established legends, such as lining up activist and DJ EvieTheCool alongside the likes of Ron Carroll or Ghettoblaster. Also look out for M-Dok's parties every other Wednesday at The Blind Barber.

21

THE BIRTH OF HOUSE MUSIC

By 1981, Frankie Knuckles had a problem. He'd been at the helm of Chicago's Warehouse club since he moved to the city in 1977, having honed his craft playing disco and salsoul in the bath houses of New York. But by 1981, disco had been declared 'dead'. Record labels were getting rid of their disco and dance departments. There were no more uptempo dance records, everything was downtempo. And the intense, spiritual crowd at the Warehouse – predominantly Black, predominantly gay, and aged between 18 and 35 – needed something new to dance to.

"That's when I realised I had to start changing certain things in order to keep feeding my dancefloor," remembered Frankie, who died in 2014, in a 1995 interview with Frank Broughton. "Or else we would have had to end up closing the club."

"So I would take different records like 'Walk The Night' by the Skatt Brothers, 'A Little Bit Of Jazz' by Nick Straker, 'Double Journey' [by Powerline] and things like that, and just completely re-edit them to make them work better for my dancefloor. Even stuff like 'I'm Every Woman' by Chaka Khan, and 'Ain't Nobody', just things like that, I'd completely re-edit them, to give my dancefloor an extra boost. I'd re-arrange them, extend them and re-arrange them."

Knuckles didn't invent the remix – the likes of Tom Moulton on the East Coast had been extending and powering up records since the '70s – but for the crowd in the Warehouse it was revolutionary. "They went for it immediately. And they would rush to the record stores the next day looking for that particular version. And never find it. It used to drive the record stores crazy." By 1983 he had added another string to his bow: laying beats over the top of tracks live, first with a rhythm maker designed for organs, and a year later with a Roland TR-909 he bought from Detroit's Derrick May. "The first time I used it, I used it on a version of 'Your Love' that I did with Jamie Principle. And I would use it live in the club. I would program different patterns into it throughout the week, and then use it throughout the course of a night, running it live, depending on the song and playing it underneath, or using it to segue between things."

Meanwhile, across the city, young DJs like Jesse Saunders at the Playground were going even further, even ditching the melodies that the Warehouse crowd loved in favour of full nights of beat tracks, while later Ron Hardy at The Music Box – home to "darker, druggier, trippier vibe," says Frankie – was experimenting with the science of playing records, live sampling parts of a track for 10 minutes at a time, pushing the crowd to the very limits.

But it was Frankie's club that gave the genre its name. Chicago radio DJs like the Hot Mix 5, who were groping for a term to describe the new sound, soon connected it to the very club where it had originated. The name gave a clarity and reality to what many have described since as 'disco's revenge': "One day I was going out south to see my god-daughter," remembers Frankie, "and we were sitting at a stop light, and on the corner there was a tavern, and in the window it had a sign that said, "WE PLAY HOUSE MUSIC". I asked this friend of mine, 'Now what is that all about?' and she said, 'It's the same stuff that you play at The Warehouse'."

Frankie Knuckles at the turntable in his Chicago home

DETROIT

Raised on Detroit's West side, Delano Smith is one of the original Detroit house DJs

A workers' city, known internationally for its picturesque urban decay and as the birthplace of Motown, P-funk and techno

It's no wonder that Detroit's low rents have attracted generations of artists and musicians – and plenty of techno tourists. There's something of a split between 'old' Detroit and some of the new arrivals, especially the tech bros and moneyed hipsters who don't integrate with the renegade spirit of the town. This is still a worker's city, where respect for venue staff is expected and flashing money around is frowned upon (most nights cost about $5 on the door anyway). Detroiters do things their own way – don't expect to discover everything that's happening on listings sites; find a local guide instead. Despite many venues closing at 2am thanks to a statewide bar service curfew, locals rarely venture out before 10. Asking 'where is everyone?' is the classic sign of an out-of-towner. Looking like you've made an effort to get dressed up is another: 'come as you are' is the dress code.

The TV Lounge (open since 1999) and the Marble Bar (opened in 2015 on the site of a former leather fetish bar) are two of the longest standing pillars of the scene. The TV Lounge is the place to find house legends like Delano Smith, Stacey Pullen and Rick Wilhite alongside international guests counting Sébastien Léger and Nastia. Look out for locals like DJ Holographic, Shigeto and Stacey 'Hotwaxx' Hale at the Marble Bar. Spot Lite Detroit, opened in 2021 by the couple behind art collective and publisher 1XRUN, is the new kid on the block: a light and airy converted industrial unit that's a combination of art space, venue and record store.

But it's the Movement Festival on Memorial Day weekend (the last Monday of May) that sees Detroit really come alive. It was founded by the sheer willpower of some of the locals in 2000 as the Detroit Electronic Music Festival, at a time when inner city techno festivals in the US were almost completely unheard of, and struggled through early funding problems and the occasional bitter artist beef to become a beacon for the city. The main 40,000-strong event is held at Hart Plaza by the riverfront, with its modernist concrete and steel sculptures in the shadow of the seven connected skyscrapers of the Renaissance Center. The festival sees the city's entire club community come together, with venues holding special events and one-off parties across the inexhaustible supply of vacant industrial space. Movement is usually curated by a local legend, with Carl Craig programming the first. A look at the line-ups over the years reveals the successive generations of DJs and producers who've come through the city, from the Belleville Three through Jeff Mills and Richie Hawtin up to Matthew Dear, MK, Claude VonStroke, Seth Troxler and Lee Curtiss.

The city itself, near bankrupt since its once all-conquering industrial base collapsed, is understandably a bit of a chequerboard, with active neighbourhoods spread out amid a sometimes pretty grim void. Public transport is limited, aside from the striking but pointless 'Detroit People Mover' robot monorail, which looks like something RoboCop's OCP corp dreamed up (and which may have inspired the famous *Simpsons* episode). If you want to switch between the districts where the action is, like Midtown and Corktown, expect to be getting a lot of Ubers.

No Way Back, Movement Festival's 14-hour afterparty

Moodymann is an eccentric original in the best Detroit tradition

DJS / LABEL

Moodymann
The enigmatic roller-skating and Prince-obsessed Kenny Dixon Jr is an eccentric original in the best Detroit tradition, whether he's creating timeless house classics like 'Shades Of Jae' and 'Don't You Want My Love' or causing much pearl clutching among dance music snobs by dropping Kings Of Leon in the middle of a festival set.

Stacey Hotwaxx Hale
The 'Godmother of House Music' Stacey Hale started DJing in the city in the '70s as a pupil of original DJ icon Ken Collier, possibly becoming one of the first women to ever beatmatch. Since then, she's become a driving force in the city's scene with her radio shows, DJing and production, and her constant championing of the city, especially with opportunities for its youth.

DJ Holographic
Described variously as a 'one-woman funk machine' and 'the future of Detroit techno', the former coat check girl at Michigan's Necto club was tapped up last year by Carl Craig to mix the latest instalment of the Detroit Love mix series, and has played everywhere from Panorama Bar to the Dirtybird Campout.

Underground Resistance
Less a record label than a manifesto for a new consciousness, 'Mad' Mike Banks and Jeff Mills's production collective took influences from Afrofuturism, sci-fi, jazz, funk and the avant-garde – as well as taking control of the means of distribution – to set out an experimental, anti-corporate, self-sufficient path for the genre. The irony of their logo becoming a commodified shorthand for rebellion on T-shirts from Birmingham to Berlin won't be lost on them.

GRiZ lights up Detroit's TV Lounge, an intimate venue offering house, techno and more

No Way Back
"The coolest place to be on this night, on this planet, in this solar system, in this galaxy," is how DJ and producer Jasen Loveland describes this annual 14-hour psychedelic-inspired Movement afterparty, run by local label Interdimensional Transmissions. Held amid the bare brick and concrete of the Tangent Gallery, it's a chance for the nation's techno subculture to celebrate the city.

○ CLUB / RECORD SHOP

Spot Lite Detroit
The owners call this new, multifaceted space a "love letter to Detroit". An emphasis on the diversity of the staff and crowd underpins a mission to be inclusive for women and Detroit's under-represented LGBTQ+ community, while the all-day opening makes this as much of a community hangout as a club venue. Look out especially for Theo Parrish's nine-hour Sunday residency.

Crowds at Detroit's Movement Festival brave torrential rain

THE ELECTRIFYING MOJO AND THE ROOTS OF TECHNO

Scientists describe Earth as a 'Goldilocks' planet, a place where conditions combined perfectly and coincidentally (not too hot, not too cold, etc.) to enable life. And so it was with techno's genesis in Detroit. The city's rich musical history, from Berry Gordy to George Clinton, played its part. As did the rise of a Black middle class, drawn by the growing automotive industry in the region, who found themselves with free time and disposable income for the first time due to its well-paid and relatively enlightened employment opportunities. The automated rhythm of those great factories surely had an influence, as did pulp sci-fi and the city's sleek modernist architecture.

But any new creation needs a catalyst. Another theory posits the spark of life as having arrived from the stars, on a meteor perhaps, or via some other galactic intervention. Something like Detroit radio DJ, The Electrifying Mojo.

Mojo's radio show began in 1977 on Detroit's WGPR and sounded like a dispatch from another planet. Playing to a racially mixed audience, which was itself something of a novelty at the time, Mojo would spin anything from the Human League to Parliament-Funkadelic to Kraftwerk. Sometimes he'd play whole album sides, or three solid hours of Prince and Michael Jackson, but he had a distinct taste for the weird and experimental.

Every show would begin with a long intro as he "landed the Mothership" on a Detroit building. The first part of his show would be full of the latest dance sounds from Detroit (the likes of Parliament-Funkadelic and Bootsy Collins) jammed up against New Wave sounds from Europe, such as Ultravox and Depeche Mode. At midnight, he would start the Midnight Funk Association segment, asking "members" (you could apply to the radio station for a membership card) to honk their horns, or turn on their porch lights, and stand up. By 1981, he was running mix competitions for local DJs, asking them to send in 15-minute mixes for the show. Most of all, by playing the coldly synthetic New Wave and Kraftwerkian sounds of Europe in a context that somehow made sense alongside the local funk, Mojo pointed out the similarities between them, the connective tissue. He called it "a journey to the bottom line of music, that combines all the grooves of the world."

Detroit had always had a huge party culture. By the '80s there was a big disco and funk scene around DJs like Ken Collier and John Collins, thriving gay clubs, and massive parties for high school kids in ballrooms and social clubs. There were DJ crews and dance squads with their own routines, named after aspirational fashion labels and sports cars. One of these crews made a song about their ideal clubber (who read *GQ*, enjoyed "fine wine and cheese" and drove a Porsche 928). They took it to The Electrifying Mojo in the winter of 1980, who played it over and over again. And although it wasn't till a few years later that sci-fi enthusiast and Mojo apprentice Juan Atkins unilaterally named the style of music he and his high school friends were making 'techno', many people reckon that 1981 record, A Number Of Names's 'Sharevari' (Charivari was a high-end New York clothing store) was the genre's first tune.

Detroit's striking industrial past forms the backdrop for the birth of techno

MIAMI

From the Beach to the Downtown, Magic City is the home of glitzy mega clubs and exciting micro scenes

There was a time when Miami could seriously consider itself the centre of the dance music world – at least for one week of the year. Before the internet, Miami's World Music Conference was where the biggest records of the year broke, with superstar DJs queuing up patiently poolside for exclusive promos. It was where the world's electronic music industry would descend each year in a blizzard of cocaine, boorish behaviour and legendary excess. It was where names were made and scores were settled, new genres surfaced, and breakthrough chart hits were signed. Later, when the likes of ADE would siphon off European dealmakers, the heat of that original superstar DJ culture had cooled and digital music had democratised distribution, 'Music Week' would belong to huge EDM festivals like Ultra, symbiotic with the descent on the city of thousands of barely dressed Spring Breakers, brosteppers and girls gone wild.

But this most European-Caribbean of American cities has always had a solid core of club culture, cycling through various districts of the city as they themselves cycle through fashionability, then commercialisation, then back again. Bottle service has driven the real thing mainly away from Miami Beach (aside from the huge LIV, the place to see DJs like Black Coffee, David Guetta and Tiësto) and into the Downtown area, home to venues like Space, which welcomes huge names every week from Seth Troxler to Dixon, and its Floyd lounge, where you'll catch the likes of Avalon Emerson and Maayan Nidam. In the Upper East Side, converted motels make for hip bars and cafés. Things

An impressive show of smoke and lights at Rakastella

get going late here – around midnight – and then keep going. Hopping from one club to another is possible as many are open until the last DJ decides to finish playing, and even then there's usually a dive bar like The Corner or Max Club Deuce where everyone will eventually end up. While the distinctive sound of Miami bass had its heyday in the '90s, house and tech house are the dominant genres now, but look out for the burgeoning queer warehouse micro scene of the Little River neighbourhood, and collectives like MASISI.

Miami Music Week has been eclipsed by Art Basel, an annual event centred around the stunning murals of Wynwood Art District in early December. The event is accompanied by a program of big underground parties with a visual arts component from the likes of DJ Tennis and Damian Lazarus – and hopefully the return of the incredible Rakastella, curated in 2021 by Innervisions and Life and Death. Year-round though, the apex of Miami's club scene remains Space Miami, still one of the best clubbing experiences in the world and a worthy successor to its Ibiza namesake.

This is a fashion-conscious city where people love to dress up to go out, and clubs make a big effort with production. Even the tiniest club in Miami has a full-time bathroom attendant, so take some cash to avoid awkwardness around the soap dispenser, and don't assume everyone here speaks English – a little bit of Spanish, or at least Spanglish, will go a long way. Of course, this is still a US city, so there is no public transport to speak of.

Danny Daze

A second generation Miamian whose mother fled Castro's Cuba at the age of five, Daze is a 'DJ's DJ' in demand worldwide and a producer of electro and techno with echoes of the Miami Bass sound. His Omnidisc label is one of the most consistent in the scene.

MASISI

This DJ/party/multimedia collective consisting of Akia Dorsainvil, Ashley Venom, and Terrell Villiers promotes the music of Miami's Island diaspora. Its mission is based on political activism, creating safe spaces and events for queer and trans people of colour, many of whom face discrimination in the city's club culture mainstream.

Schematic Music Company

Schematic was founded by Romulo Del Castillo and Joshua Kay in 1996 as a post-rave home listening label, and quickly became known as 'America's Warp', releasing artists such as Phoenecia and Push Button Objects, and renowned for artwork created by pioneering graphic designers.

CLUBS

Do Not Sit On The Furniture

A quirky, much-loved holdout against the bottle service culture that has captured most of Miami Beach, this beachside bunker (owned and run by well-respected DJ, Behrouz, and wife Megan) is dominated by a huge mirror ball chandelier and favours DJs from the deeper, organic end of house and techno, from stables like Anjunadeep and All Day I Dream.

Space Miami

While it regularly welcomes the biggest international names in electronic music, the residents are a hugely important reason as to why this giant 2,500 capacity warehouse-style venue (with a roof terrace) continues to lead the way in Magic City. Look out especially for new arrival from New York Layla Benitez on the bill: her dark disco, '80s influenced sound is a perfect fit for Miami's Vaporwave vibe.

O RECORD SHOP

Sweat records

This pastel-painted indie in Little Haiti was co-founded by DJ Lauren Reskin and specialises in new and used vinyl and DJ equipment, as well as in-store events and parties across various Miami venues.

Get Lost festival, the pinnacle event of Miami Music Week

LAS VEG AS

Monument-building on a pharaonic scale meets a new generation of neighbourhood style-clubbing amid the neon

The EDM wave has started to roll back in Las Vegas, and it has left behind something very surprising. In this city of constant reinvention, with a ruthless focus on the bottom line, where often spectacle is substance, the idea that Vegas could build an actual underground scene seemed a pipe dream. But now... On the strip, where every major casino complex seems to be anchored by a $100m dollar nightclub (and a DJ-led pool party), house and techno DJs have joined the ranks of Calvin Harris, Alesso, Steve Aoki and Zedd with residencies and regular appearances. On any given week you might find Black Coffee playing the Marquee club at Cosmopolitan, Carl Cox playing Moonbeam at the shiny new Zouk, or RL Grime playing XS at Encore.

Of course, these clubs are ever more expensive to get into, with a 'millionaires-on-a-stag-do' vibe still rooted in bottle service, fuelling an ever-escalating arms race of DJ fees. Then again, they are also spectacular. The newest kid on the block is Moonbeam, a Tulum temple themed cavern attached to Resort World. Its 41,000-square-foot day club, AYU, is custom-built for parties around the horseshoe-shaped main pool, featuring a stage, a giant LED screen, a 2,874-strong capacity, and private pools, shady cabanas and winding pathways through tropical greenery. Marquee, on the second floor of the Cosmopolitan, holds 5,000, has an LED wall that is quite probably visible from space, seven different bars and three rooms. XS at Encore and Hakkasan at MGM are monuments built on a scale not seen since the pharaohs. The TAO nightclub at The Venetian is more intimate, with a calculated decadence including lingerie-clad dancers in cages and bathtubs, a sound system designed by NYC legend John Lyons, and DJs with names like Four Color Zack and Justin Credible.

But there is life beyond the strip. Over the past couple of years, an influx of people to the north and west of the city – from California in particular – has changed the demographic: younger, hipper, and with more appetite for modern, urban neighbourhood living as opposed to strip malls and McMansions. AFTER's Thom Svast has been repping the underground in Vegas for decades, laying out a set of 'DJ rules' ("do not play a pre-mixed set, do not say a fucking word on the microphone" – a cry of ironic existential despair at the superficiality of club culture in the city), which went viral in 2014. But Vegas is finally starting to catch up.

Corner Bar Management, an ambitious multi venue project, is transforming the formerly rundown Fremont neighbourhood, nestled up next to the Arts

District, into a new nexus for electronic music. Bringing together club crews new and old that have kept the fires of authenticity burning – Club Soda, MNTRA, Elation, RVLTN, Holy House – and centred around new venues We All Scream and Discopussy, club nights and brunch parties here offer viable alternatives for when the LED screens bring on a migraine or your eyes start to sting from the pool parties. The rules still apply everywhere in Vegas clubland though: pace yourself in this land of day drinking, tip well, and, most importantly, respect the staff's boundaries and don't ever ask them where you can find drugs. Or you'll quickly find yourself back out, alone, on the neon-lit streets.

Jaw-dropping spectacle at Electric Daisy Carnival

A colourful dancefloor at Discopussy

DJS

MNTRA
DJ trio Oscar Molina, Lance Le Rock and Bad Beat make up MNTRA, whose 'Techno Taco Tuesdays' have long had a cult following in the city. Catch their techno and tech house sets at TTT's new home, Lucky Day, on East Fremont Street.

Skye
Originally from Dallas, Skye began as a pro dancer in some of the biggest venues in Vegas before becoming a resident at clubs including Drai's and playing events like Soul State. Developing a grooving style that spans tech house, house and techno, she's also released on labels Unnamed & Unknown and Innocent Music.

CLUB / EVENT

Discopussy
A new 500-cap Fremont space inspired by clubs in London, New York and Detroit, Discopussy is notable for the pin-sharp Void sound system, residencies from DJs like Claude VonStroke, Gettoblaster and Bad Boy Bill, and a giant light sculpture of an octopus that takes up almost the entire ceiling (this is still Vegas, after all).

Electric Daisy Carnival
Held on the giant Las Vegas speedway, this three day riot of breathtakingly elaborate, gigantic stages, funfair, fireworks and 134,000 ravers per day has a line-up featuring every name in EDM (from deadmau5 b2b Kaskade to A-Trak to Tiesto) plus scores more, from Honey Dijon to Sub Focus and Tale of Us to TSHA. The biggest, brightest event on the US festival calendar.

PAUL OAKENFOLD

Has any figure in dance music ever taken bigger gambles – and won – than Paul Oakenfold? Fresh from Ibiza in '88, he booked London's biggest club at the time, Heaven, on a *Monday night* for his Spectrum parties when the nascent Balearic/acid house scene consisted of a few dozen enthusiasts, persevering until the city (and later the country) caught up. A few years later, he helped a glut of indie artists like The Stone Roses and Happy Mondays to fuse their sound with acid house rhythms as the house purists scoffed. He turned his back on his world-famous (and highly lucrative) residency at Liverpool's Cream in 1998 just when it seemed at its peak, to take his 'brand' global. He made overtures to Hollywood, producing soundtracks for blockbuster movies when such an idea was unheard of for electronic artists. And, of course, he turned Las Vegas into a hotspot for dance music.

In 2008, when Oakie started his residency at Rain (a since-closed nightclub attached to the Palms Casino and Hotel), the competing residencies in the city were the likes of Sonny & Cher, comedian Carrot Top, and Donny Osmond. Elvis may have reinvented himself there, but generally Vegas was where clapped-out acts who'd seen better days went to prepare for retirement. There were clubs and a legacy of desert raves, but frankly, Oakenfold's claims that Vegas could be 'America's Ibiza' were met with disbelief and even mockery at the time.

And maybe Oakenfold was the only person who could've done it. Few DJs at the time had his level of recognition in the US, thanks to two decades of touring, huge mix compilations, collabs with people like Madonna, Hollywood links, and his pioneering 'proper albums'. Combined with the showmanship of Vegas – inflatables, acrobats, and more lasers than a battalion of Stormtroopers – and the city's untapped reservoir of young locals and holidaymakers, the event quickly became a smash. Record attendances saw him rebooked by the club for another two years. But more importantly, the success of 'Perfecto Vegas' saw the entire city double down on dance music. Other casinos started looking for their own equivalent, with Kaskade – a figurehead for a new generation of US artists after his work with deadmau5 on chart smash 'I Remember' – becoming a crucial pioneer at Marquee. Over the next decade, whole new multi-billion dollar casinos and hotels were launched, joining original outlier Pure at Ceasar's Palace by putting their club offering front and centre, on a scale of investment unmatched anywhere

Paul Oakenfold took his brand global in 1998, starting with a move to Hollywood

on the planet. Regular DJ-led pool parties would become the norm everywhere. The colossal EDC festival would move to Vegas, transforming the city into a huge rave spectacle every year. Vegas would become a huge cash cow for DJs from the US and beyond, with fees escalating wildly across the world, pricing out some of them from anything but the biggest US festivals or glitziest clubs.

And while club culture changed Vegas, Vegas also changed club culture. This being a city where return on investment is calculated to the last cent, the casinos wanted their 'vig'. Bottle service, hostesses, Dante's Inferno-like concentric circles of VIP areas, and anything else that could justify exorbitant drinks prices would start in Vegas and infiltrate clubs everywhere. DJ sets were even analysed and dissected for how they affected bottle sales, with those who could ratchet up the cash registers with the right tempo and timing of their 'drops' rewarded accordingly, affecting even the way electronic music was produced. Oakenfold moved on from Rain after three years, having transformed the scene yet again. Whether he changed it for the better hardly matters. No one gambles bigger, or wins more often.

LOS ANGE LES

Rooftop glam, celebrity promoters and Downtown warehouse parties in the California megalopolis

LA's brutal traffic, vast distances and 2am closing time means club hopping here is not an option. In fact, should you fancy hitting a bar or two before going to a club (something rare among the locals), find somewhere in the same area as the venue. Perhaps it's because of this that LA's club scene has often seemed a little fragmented, with crowds tending to be loyal to one or two promotions. In LA, the promoter is king (or queen). Figures like Insomniac's Pasquale Rotella and HARD's Gary Richards are bona fide celebrities, with social media followings that often outshine venues and even their own club brands. Many of them, like Richards (as Destructo) and Heidi Lawden, are also DJs, which helps.

Drum'n'bass Thursday weekly Respect has been pushing the genre in the city for an astonishing 23 years now, cycling through multiple generations of clubbers while becoming the priority stop for international deebee talent in the US. So dank with weed smoke that it's difficult to know when you're inside and when you're in its buzzing outdoor area, its current home is Station 1640 in Hollywood. A newer event with an equally loyal following is proudly pansexual extravaganza, A Club Called Rhonda. Famed for its incredible themed venue transformations, inspired by historic clubs like Studio 54, Danceteria and Paradise Garage, Rhonda aims to "put sleaze on a pedestal" and attracts artists from Nina Kraviz and 2manydjs to pop star Robyn, alongside its strong line-up of local resident talent.

Downtown, so long the hub for LA's illegal rave scene, has recently come to prominence for legit clubbing thanks to frequent warehouse parties and venues such as Exchange, but non-driving visitors should be wary of wandering into the heartbreaking decrepitude of nearby Skid Row. Hollywood remains home to the historic Avalon and new club Academy, with its warehouse-like main room and outdoor patio; both venues have more of an EDM/trance vibe. Hollywood is also home to Sound, a 500-cap venue opened in 2012 that was one of the first to reject the EDM juggernaut and focus resolutely on building a community around underground talent. Arguably, it is Sound (along with Low End Theory) that showed the way for the rest of the city to reject the Vegas model and follow its own path. Meanwhile non profit radio station Dublab plays an influential role in shaping the city's underground sound.

While large scale outdoor events are rare, mainly thanks to a Byzantine licensing regime that requires about 18 months of work to throw a party in a public space, look for one-offs in the pedestrianised Chinatown. There is also a healthy – if sometimes glitzy – hotel rooftop and pool party scene, spearheaded by promoters like Wicked Paradise and Soho House. LA's also not too far from Coachella, where one breakthrough set can still supercharge a career.

DJ Harvey

He may only play in the city once a year, but English émigré Harvey is arguably the city's favourite DJ, building a rep here the old-fashioned way: by overstaying his visa and being unable to tour internationally for a decade until he'd secured a green card. His warm, chugging electro and disco – the aural equivalent of a golden hour photo filter – is a perfect fit for LA.

Heidi Lawden

Another Brit expat, Lawden is a driving force behind LA's recent club renaissance, both as Harvey's manager and as a DJ and promoter with teammates Jeniluv and Masha Mar. The trio hold regular warehouse and club parties and launched the ambitious boutique festival Dusk Camp in 2019 in the wilderness south of the city.

Skrillex

He may rarely play the city these days, but Skrillex is very much a part of LA's recent story. The DJ moved back to the city as a teenager to try to make it as a musician in goth and emo bands before experiencing an epiphany watching Daft Punk's epochal performance at Coachella in 2007. With more Grammys than any other electronic artist and an oeuvre that ranges from festival-conquering 'brostep' to acclaimed collabs with the likes of Boys Noize and Four Tet, he remains, for many, the face of electronic music in the US.

Dim Mak

Before spearheading the kind of hyperactive electro that would later morph into an EDM juggernaut (think Bloody Beetroots, MSTRKRFT), Steve Aoki's record label made its bones championing indie dance tastemakers such as The Kills, Gossip, and Bloc Party back in the early '00s, and his Dim Mak Tuesday parties in the city became the hottest ticket on the West Coast. His eye always on the next prize, Aoki has recently diversified into Latin sounds with offshoot Dim Mak En Fuego.

Exchange Los Angeles

Built inside the imposing Moderne splendour of LA's former stock exchange, this four-floor 1,500-cap venue opened in 2015 after a delicate two-year build. Fully kitted out with directional lighting and LED screens, it's a fittingly hi-tech arena for visiting European techno behemoths including Sven Väth and Patrick Topping.

Skrillex, considered by many as the face of electronic music in the US

Laser beams over the dancefloor of Exchange in downtown LA

43

LA legend DJ Harvey

○ RECORD SHOP

Amoeba

In a city that tends to bulldoze its history without compunction, and in a world where record shops have become an endangered species, somehow Amoeba has survived to become a Hollywood landmark since opening on Sunset Boulevard all the way back in 2001. Well, until recently. A new location opened in 2021; while it lacks the iconic neon facade, it's still, they claim, the largest independent record store in the world. A treasure trove.

LOW END THEORY

Every so often a club night aligns perfectly with an explosion of local creativity and genuine musical innovation, and a scene is born around it. A Wednesday night, 400-cap event held in a grimy venue in the slightly down-at-heel neighbourhood of Lincoln Heights, Low End Theory was the unlikely birthplace of a new sound.

Growing out of the Sketchbook club, where local producers inspired by pioneers like J Dilla (who died the same year LET opened) would swap tapes and inspiration, LET began similarly, as a place for producers and DJs to play music to each other ("If you were going, chances are you were playing too," remembers regular Tokimonsta). A few years after its founding in 2006, though, Low End Theory had become the most exciting club in the US, attracting the likes of Erykah Badu and Thom Yorke to play, being championed by Mary Anne Hobbs on BBC Radio One alongside the likes of FWD>> in London, and even visited by Prince once (albeit for a few minutes).

For perhaps the first time, LA underground club culture had something that was truly its own, not a facsimile or transplant of a template from New York or London or Detroit. The crowd was as much a melting pot as the city. While the creators point to the role that the rise of medical marijuana played in the scene, it was musical, not narcotic, experimentation that fuelled Low End Theory. Crowd-surfing and moshing were common on the packed, smoky floor as DJs and producers, liberated by the revolution in software-based production, connected the dots between psych and experimental rock, jazz, hip-hop, the nascent 90bpm dubstep sound, techno, and broken beat.

The list of DJs and artists who made their name at LET is legion and includes the likes of Tokimonsta, Dedalus, The Glitch Mob and Nosaj Thing, but it was Dilla protege Flying Lotus, honorary 'sixth resident' and an attendee since the Sketchbook club days, who would become most synonymous – his debut album 'Los Angeles' was as much a tribute to the club as to his hometown.

Perhaps without the trailblazing of Low End Theory running interference, there wouldn't have been the explosion of commercial 'brostep' that powered US festivals for long enough to make the name dubstep almost a dirty word. But then neither would there have been the explosion of low-end experimentation that has come to shape modern music and progress hip-hop into new realms.

The club came to a sour and abrupt end almost overnight in 2018 when sexual assault allegations against founder member William 'The Gaslamp Killer' Bensussen surfaced online, but its legacy and its impact on music can still be heard, from Kendrick Lamar's 'To Pimp A Butterfly' to the new jazz and soul of Thundercat and Kamasi Washington, and the Soundcloud rap scene.

TORONTO

Virtual events gone IRL, a very secretive warehouse scene and a global cross pollination of sounds: Toronto's nightlife is a little more complicated these days

At the zenith of the rave days, Toronto was indisputably a clubbing capital. From 1995 to 2001, the planet's top DJs played for audiences in the tens of thousands at parties every weekend, in the city and outdoors. Roxy Blu and the Guvernment were the two bastions for the scene, kicking open their doors in the late '90s just as the city was cracking down on its booming illegal scene.

Both would cement Toronto's reputation as an international clubbing destination and become seminal to the history of clubbing in what local Drake calls 'the 6ix' (it was originally six cities). More than 12 million punters would tear up the dancefloor at the Guvernment nightclub complex while DJs like Carl Cox blessed the boards. Junglist-dominated raves there had Fabio on the roof, Andy C and ShyFX in one room, and Die and Krust playing B2B. Hype, Calibre, Daft Punk, Chemical Brothers, The Knife, Portishead, Prodigy and Underworld all made appearances. Even Bowie and Prince sometimes stormed the stage. Elsewhere, Roxy Blu's DIY spirit championed parties without compromise and became a pivotal place where marginalized people found both community and liberation deep into the night. But the momentum could not be maintained, and the crowds died down. Eventually, Toronto's rave days would be drowned out by bottle service, million-pound EDM DJs with a $30-$50 cover charge, dress codes, and more curfews.

Time, and a pandemic, actually proved positive for the scene. Club Quarantine began their virtual streaming parties in 2020 and became a global phenomenon as well as a record label. The collective, co-founded by four queer Torontonians, provided virtual hedonism for the bored and locked-down worldwide. Charlie XCX. and Kim Petras got in on the online action before Lady Gaga asked the platform to debut her album, *Chromatica* (2020).

The electronic music community has returned to clubbing IRL at full force with a heady mix of progressive promoters, DJs and producers. Ciel's event series Work In Progress brings dynamic sets that traverse the spectrum of techno, jungle, UK tech house, off-kilter breakbeat and acid, helmed by women, queer, and BIPOC producers and selectors. Club Quarantine is hosting parties at Toronto's 400-capacity former goth den The Velvet Underground by linking up with queer Latinx collective DISCOÑO. Many nights will showcase a spectrum of electronic genres on their dancefloor. There's a dynamic blend of audiences and styles of music, from the It's Not U It's Me house music parties to maximalist techno and experimental noise via Toronto's own E-Saggila. There are deep Caribbean and Asian influences, rich Eastern European roots, and Bhangra, Latin and junglist DJs.

Canada's notoriously strict curfew means most clubs close at 2am, and locals can be extremely secretive about Toronto's warehouse raves and after hours parties. Pick your moment to grill the locals on your night of choice, or even DM a few DJs or collectives personally beforehand.

Grab a bite to eat before a night out around hip neighbourhoods like Parkdale, Dundas West, or Kensington Market, and you'll experience the same cultural fusion that characterises the city's soundtrack. Check out Island Foods for the Caribbean, Papa Spicy for Chinese BBQ or Hanmoto for Japanese. For those searching for harder dance music and a hit of the local vibe, start your night off with a drink at Bambi's, a frequent haunt for music heads, the crews behind new-gen nights spearheading Toronto's scene, and DJs like Andrew Ross and Yu Su.

DJS / LABEL

Ciel
Xi'an-born, Toronto-based producer and DJ Ciel is a powerhouse of technical prowess. She regularly delights crowds across the world with her intricate mix of bass, jungle, techno and old skool trance classics. Despite boasting prime slots at the huge international stages of Berghain, Love International and Movement Detroit, the Discwoman signee (whose real name is Cindy Li) has remained a mainstay of her adopted home. Throwing parties such as Work in Progress and curating the collective Parallel Minds, she has positioned herself as a forward-thinking vehicle for progressive electronic sounds in the Ontario capital.

E-Sagglia
Iraq-born, Toronto-based producer and DJ Rita Mikhael – aka E-Saggila – approaches music with the same surgical precision she applied to her medical degree. She fuses visceral ambient with heart-thumping hardware techno, noise, and breakcore. She's built a solid catalogue of EPs and LPs, for Bank Records, Northern Electronics, Opal Tapes and Night Void, and toured everywhere from Trance Party at Corsica Studios in London to Zhao Dai in Beijing.

Parallel Minds
Parallel Minds is a collective of like-minded musicians, DJs and graphic artists coming together to create a label and spread Toronto dance music to the rest of the world. Their inaugural release, *Parallel Minds Vol. 1*, features cloudy, off-kilter club sizzlers full of jolting

rhythms and heavy bass plumes from co-founder Daniel 58, foggy bass and skittering electronics from Yohei S., and a B-side by Raf Reza's alias Radiant Aural Faculty: a vibrant mixture of Hindi vocal samples layered meticulously in between freaked-out synths and thumping breakbeat drum, all representative of Toronto's abilities to crisscross cultures.

CLUBS

Sub Division
This underground eatery and electronic music venue is located beneath the Rabbit! Rabbit! Rabbit! restaurant on King Street West. They encourage visitors to wear T-shirts, jeans, sneakers and whatever's comfortable to dance in, as well as strictly enforcing a phone ban to encourage engagement with each other, the space, the music and the environment. Since relaunching in 2022, they've hosted the UK's own Bradley Zero with his Rhythm Section party, and a staggering local line-up including Nitin, a formidable house heavyweight, and Jeremy P. Caulfield, a key figure in Toronto's techno scene, alongside former Canadian B-Boy turned DJ and producer Ali Black, playing Chicago-influenced footwork and house.

CODA
From the beginning, CODA has emphasised local talent, be that the Canadian-made 50,000+ watt sound system or the home-grown DJs they book alongside an international line-up. It's a 550-cap club in a classic dancefloor-flanked-by-bars mould, and prides itself on a welcoming ego-free crowd. The exciting programming includes Seth Troxler going b2b with Canadian legend Tiga, and Chippy Nonstop's frenetic Pep Rally parties where techno meets playful rave and 160bpm pop.

○ RECORD SHOP

Invisible City
Invisible City has the most meticulously curated selection of rare Caribbean funk, soca, and island soul records in Toronto. Browsing through the shop's stock feels like you're getting a detailed musical history lesson from an experienced elder. It's complemented by a generous selection of mutant dance, electronic soul, meditative new age, and Paradise Garage-era disco, which the Invisible City Editions reissue label sits perfectly alongside – and a $5 bin that you can't miss.

Ciel performing at a rave in Toronto

MON TREAL

The most European
of Canadian cities
comes alive with
outdoor parties,
Piknics and festivals
when the spring
thaw finally begins

Ravers brave the snow at Montreal's chilliest outdoor festival, Igloofest

"Montreal has always been known as a party city," says legendary Montreal-based DJ and producer Tiga, "not just across Canada, but with people visiting from the US, Boston, New York, Vermont. You can drink at 18 here, younger than the US and even other states like Ontario." Combined with a progressive, European atmosphere thanks to its French heritage, liberal laws on cannabis and the sex trade, a huge gay scene, and a club culture that comes alive every Spring in a riot of festivals and outdoor events, it's no wonder.

Montreal was a major disco town in the '70s, home to record labels like Unidisc and acts like Gino Soccio and Lime. A New York-style club culture and warehouse scene blossomed in the '80s. "Then," says Tiga, in the early '90s, "rave hit and the scene exploded: between big organised raves and huge afterhours clubs open all night, I think it was the biggest scene in North America. Giant clubs with great sound systems and so many DJs coming in from all over the world."

The days of giant raves every weekend may have ended in the early '00s, but Montreal's nightlife has matured into something different, yet no less special. The club scene is kept smouldering year-round by the legendary Stereo, described by Canadian DJ Sydney Blu as "not only one of the best venues in Canada, [but] also arguably the best in North America"; Datcha, a Russian themed intimate spot to grab a drink to the sounds of funk, disco and electro; and New City Gas, a historic remnant of the industrial era, formerly housing a council gasification plant for Montreal's city lighting and now showcasing guests like Eric Prydz and Armin van Buuren. There are also event spaces like MTELUS and Ausgang Plaza, the latter of which has hosted DJs from DâM-FunK to Jacques Greene. Known to locals as the Metropolis, MTELUS is the

⬡ RECORD SHOP

La Rama
Combining a clubhouse feel with a breathtaking selection of electronic records, from Japanese ambient to Jungle, La Rama has become world-famous. It's also a community hub for Montreal's club and electronic scene.

Canadian-Haitian DJ Kaytranada performing in 2016

spot to catch big name acts from Vampire Weekend to Hot Chip, plus DJ-led night Nocturne, which features names like Blawan, Mathew Jonson, Jlin, Nicola Cruz, Wajatta and more. Igloofest, one of the world's chilliest outdoor raves, packs in the names at the Old Port docks in February.

But it's after the spring thaw that Montreal really comes alive. "Winter can be pretty gruesome," Tiga explains. "Below 25°F [-3.8°C] outside, snowstorms, weeks of slush. So spring and summer in Montreal are incredible. You spent months and months and months just waiting and when spring comes it's this crazy catharsis." Piknic Électronik, a short ferry ride from the Old Port, hosts chilled Sunday afternoon-to-evening sets from house and techno names like Loco Dice, Dusky, Soul Clap, Dam Swindle, Octo Octa and dozens more on two stages. The MUTEK music and digital arts festival, with more than 100 artists from the experimentalist edge (think Philippe Vandal and Alexis Langevin-Tétrault), happens late summer every year, and there are dozens more outdoor events to choose from once Spring has sprung.

DJS / CREW / LABEL

Kaytranada
Bursting onto the scene with a handful of unique remixes on Soundcloud that were unlike anything heard before, Kaytranada clocked up millions of plays with his flips of Janet Jackson's 'If', Teedra Moses's 'Be Your Girl' and Jill Scott's 'Golden', all loaded with the bumps and whomps that have come to characterise his sound. His debut album 99.9% – a 15-track collection of swagger-dripping r'n'b, hip-hop, soul and funk, featuring guests such as Anderson .Paak, Craig David and Karriem Riggins – was *Mixmag*'s Album of the Year in 2014.

Misstress Barbara
A pillar of Montreal's house and techno scene since she started DJing in the city in the late '90s, Italian-born Barbara Bonfiglio is also the producer and singer-songwriter behind two artist albums. She was one of the first internationally known female DJs and is continuing to inspire to women in the business today, within Canada and beyond.

Moonshine
Co-founded by Montreal Afrohouse artist Pierre Kwenders in 2014, the Moonshine collective throw underground parties and art events on the Saturday after every full moon. After building notoriety in their native city, they've been championed at home and abroad with shows in places such as France, Belgium, Italy, the US and Chile.

Turbo Records
Montreal is justifiably proud of Turbo. Founded by Tiga in 1998, it's been integral to the careers of a raft of incredible artists ever since. The label includes Gesaffelstein, Duke Dumont, locals Chromeo, and, more recently, ANNA and Charlotte de Witte. Genres range from pure techno to house, electro to pop. Turbo also releases Tiga's own productions and collaborations with Zombie Nation, as ZZT.

CLUB

Stereo
Equipped with a hydraulic floor, a meticulously double-layered sound wall, and a top of the line sound system designed by the prolific Angel Moraes (who honed his craft at Paradise Garage), Stereo is Montreal's most famous club. The afterhours opens at 2am and on a big weekend at Stereo, you can catch DJs like Hernán Cattáneo, Guy J, Nicole Moudaber, Chus & Ceballos, Carlo Lio and Nathan Barato play all night long. Ostrich, Simply City and Jesse Zotti are among the few Montreal locals that hold residencies.

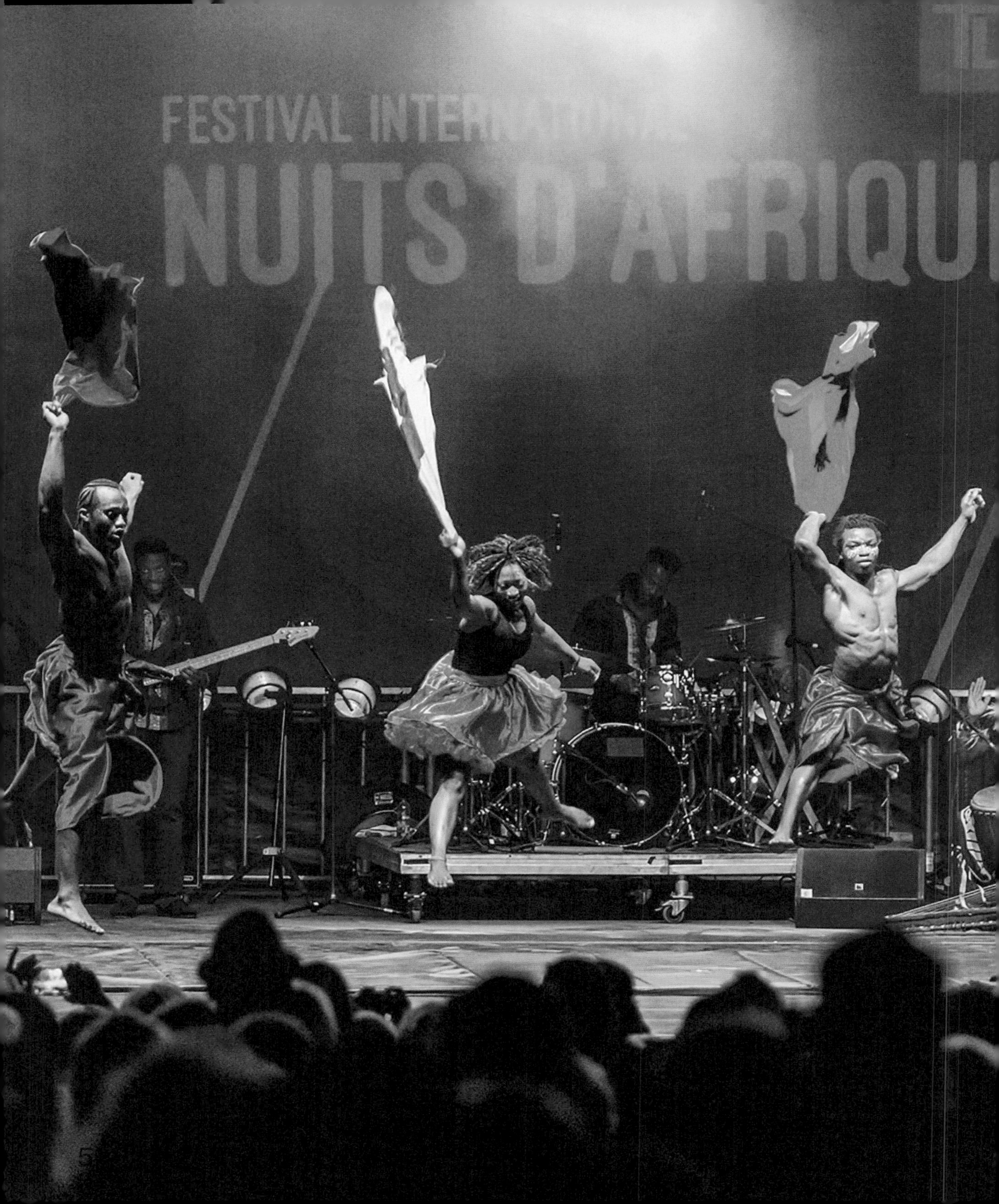
FESTIVAL
NUITS

NUITS D'AFRIQUE

Besides its house and techno clubs and festivals, Montreal is an unlikely epicentre of Afro-Caribbean music and club culture, celebrated annually since 1987 by Nuits D'Afrique. Quebec is the only French-speaking province in Canada, long attracting immigrants from Francophone countries in Africa and the Caribbean. The largest minority in the city are Haitians (home-grown hero Kaytranada is half-Haitian) followed by West Africans from French-speaking countries such as Senegal, Côte d'Ivoire, Mali and Congo. Each diaspora has brought their culture, traditions and, most importantly of all, their music to the city.

"Our founder, Lamine Touré, comes from Guinea, and an era where culture was very important," says Festival International Nuits d'Afrique (FINA) Director Suzanne Rousseau. "We reach out to communities via local radio and universities, and those [channels] are just as important to us as national or mass media. The great thing about our scenes and festivals is that they're not really separated, they all blend naturally. It's too small a city to have a separation between scenes." Rousseau and her team strive to represent as many different nations in as many genres as possible: "It's multi-generational via Africa, but we also book from nations that have been directly influenced by Africa, like the French and English Caribbean for example, as well as Latin America. We've been doing this ever since our first edition."

Indeed, Nuits D'Afrique has become a major destination for the biggest names in African and African-inspired music, booking everyone from Nigerian royalty like Femi Kuti to the 'Golden Voice of Africa', Mali's Salif Keita. Events are spread across 13 days of indoor show and six days of outdoor events, and are centred on Montreal's Parterre du Quartier des spectacles, a 1 sq km cultural area consisting of eight public spaces, and some 40 performance theatres and bar areas.

While the festival certainly plays an important role as an annual showcase to the world, its venues like the 35-year-old Club Balattou – founded by Touré as a "ball for all", and the club from which the festival grew – that keep the scene strong the rest of the year. "It's a virtuous circle for creativity," says Poirier, a producer, DJ and club promoter who has released on Ninja Tune, and who puts on monthly shows in Montreal (Qualité De Luxe) and DJ sets across the world dedicated to Afrobeats and dancehall hits. "Singers or producers see a party and get inspired, and a series of monthly, even weekly raves ends up becoming a scene."

Nuits D'Afrique, a major destination for big names in African and African-inspired music

São Paulo

Ciudad de México

Río de Ja

Santiago

Chapter 2

CENTRAL & SOUTH AMERICA

arina

santiago

Buenos Aires

Ciudad de México

Río de Jan

Rio de J

de México

Montevideo

Monte

Buenos Aires

Santa Catarina

Montevideo

Santiago

Buenos Aire

MEXICO CITY

The megacity's scene is driven by crews and collectives in hip areas like Roma and Condesa

⊙ RECORD SHOPS

Roma / Revancha / retroactivo
Grab a coffee at café Delirio in Roma Norte, then hit up the selection of record shops dotted around the hip area. Start out at Roma Records for pricey vinyl cuts. Crate dig at Revancha through their heavy hi- hop selection, rare jazz and afro-beats. Then pick up a bargain at retroactivo records.

Unlike the EDM mega clubs of Cancún or the deep house superstar playground of Tulum, club culture in Mexico City (or better still "CDMX" for Ciudad de Mexico) has been compared to places like Brooklyn and Berlin: forward-looking, innovative, and often driven by marginalised communities with a strong focus on creating a new and distinctive identity for their hometown, resisting colonialism while absorbing outside influence. That trend arguably started with N.A.A.F.I (No Ambition And Fuck-all Interest), a collective and record label that began pushing the boundaries of the CDMX club scene with their wild parties in 2010. N.A.A.F.I's producers and DJs took cues from drum'n'bass , techno, Mexican hip-hop, and South African house, but also shared a fascination with the traditional and folk styles of Latin America – brass-heavy banda, rolling reggaeton, and the near-ubiquitous rhythm of cumbia. The result was musical innovation and club nights filled with both writhing mosh pits and voguing, which have propelled the rest of the scene to follow suit.

This is a truly massive megacity, so it is best to concentrate on hip neighbourhoods like Roma and Condesa (walking distance apart) to feel the vibe for yourself. Hit dive mezcal bar La Clandestina in Condesa for a shot, then grab a few of the city's signature pastor tacos from a street truck for a couple of pesos. The club scene is mostly dead Sunday through Wednesday, but Thursday to Saturday, nightlife comes alive and clubs are open until 5am, while more free-form parties usually run until 7am.

Another important collective is Chingona Sound, Mexico's first women-led sound system and DJ collective, which came together in 2022, appearing at outdoor events and protests across the city. Queer, women and BIPOC focused parties are often the hottest ticket in town, so look out for EXT's Oblivion parties, which bring together a number of crews and collectives under one umbrella, inviting international guests that have counted Legowelt and Aurora Halal.

You should also keep an eye out for LAPI at YuYu Club, or nights thrown by progressive label and collaborative Ediciones Tecpatl at venues across the city. The Fünk club – located on Insurgentes, the longest avenue in Mexico City – is a hotspot for international acts such as Daphni, Ben UFO and Chrissy, but pay attention to their Thursday night Disco Fetish parties. 350-capacity Bar Oriente, an avant-garde electronic and live music club mainly focused on nu disco and house, also has a private karaoke room with DJ cabin rental, private bar and locker room, where you can play at being headliner for the night.

In terms of festivals, Montreal's MUTEK has a regular Mexico City outpost, and Dimensions visited in 2018 with Moodymann, but the big international events are still finding their feet after lockdown. Check out Ceremonia Festival in Mexico City in the spring. This annual event typically boasts an artist line-up of 50 per cent women, as well as a strong non-binary and queer presence, and aims to join the dots between Latinx avant-pop acts like Tainy and Nathy Peluso and techno and hip-hop artists like Arca, Erika de Casier, Bicep and Wu-Tang Clan.

Mexico City's underground scene tends to be inclusive, welcoming and friendly, and locals expect that to be reciprocated. "Being respectful is the best way to make friends in Mexico City and seem trustworthy," says N.A.A.F.I. co-founder and DJ, Fausto Bahía. "We like to have a good time and keep things fun and calm between everyone. If a tourist is being an asshole, it pisses everyone off. Don't go around bothering strangers." But why would you? The chance of entry to the invitation-only MN Roy club in Roma, a unique indoor timber pyramid where people like Moscoman, Acid Pauli and Tobias Thomas have played, is worth turning on the charm for.

DJS / LABEL

DJ Puma
Over the past decade, Puma, aka Regina Pozo, has touched every part of the industry in the city. There's her early work with MUTEK, her collaborations with iconic labels like Kompakt and Cómeme, her role as one of the first DJs to write critically on New Mexican music, and her long-standing radio show on Ibero 90.9 FM. She ran an independent platform called STUDIO, where she pioneered local and international electronic music programming for millions of Mexico City residents every week. Her DJ sets, a nuanced mix of old-school house, disco, deep house, and techno explorations have seen her play for House of Vans, N.A.A.F.I, the Panther Room in NYC, and as the most broadcasted Mexican DJ talent in Boiler Room, Mexico – not forgetting her residency at YuYu.

Wasted Fates
Another pioneer in the N.A.A.F.I crew, Wasted Fates tore the dancefloor apart in 2018 at his debut in Berlin's Funkhaus as he unleashed a mosh-pit maelstrom of cross-pollinated club styles, blending booming trap bass with skittering percussion, fragments of Latin instruments, and triplet rhythms. A good feel for his music can be found on his *Turbio* EP, a dark concoction of dembow, dancehall and grime.

Infinite Machine
Marrying experimental sounds from around the world, loosely themed around the neo-punk movement, Infinite Machine has cultivated a community of disruptive and pioneering artists from Mexico and beyond. The label celebrated its tenth year of pushing barriers and redefining club music in 2021 by releasing a club-focused decade anniversary compilation, featuring contributions from Galtier, Laughing Ears, YILAN, Renslink, Sha Ru, Xiao Quan, Benfika and Daniel Ruane.

CLUB / EVENT

YuYu
Yu Yu is situated in La Juárez, a vibrant area of the Cuauhtémoc neighbourhood known for its youth culture and creativity. The club is a subterranean 120-capacity space with a cocktail bar and record store attached. Lush red movie seats line the back of the dancefloor, which is drenched in a blood-red neon light and accompanied by a phenomenal sound system. It's a good place to check out local selectors and catch rare international sets up close. Expect everything from bass-laden techno to house, ballroom to psychedelic electro-cumbia, with artists like Jasmine Infiniti, Dengue Dengue Dengue and Chippy Nonstop.

Ediciones Tecpatl
Collaborative and inclusive promoters and record label Tecpatl host a diverse range of rising CDMX new-gen talent at venues across the city. Here you might find Arieshandmodel, one of the most interesting local female selectors on the scene, go b2b with Bruja Prieta, a trans, non-binary spiritual artist, activist and blistering hot DJ. You can also catch international DJs who don't roll through Mexico every day, such as Lisbon's DJ Nigga Fox.

A party organised by EXT Collective in a beautiful historic building in downtown Mexico City

RIO DE JANEIRO

Nomadic parties dominate the scene in Rio, transforming locations from seaside kiosks to the slopes of the Sugar Loaf

⦿ RECORD SHOP

Facchi Records
A true collection of rarities and first-rate vinyl novelties in Lapa, curated by Rodrigo Facchinetti. Here you can find everything from gems of Brazilian dance music and house and disco classics to vintage sound equipment. The store has become a hotspot for local DJs.

Known as the 'Marvelous City', Rio de Janeiro is a kind of cultural and scenic microcosm of Brazil. Land of samba, bossa nova and funk carioca, the city also has a musical history linked to pop, rock and electronic music. Clubs like Bunker 94, Dama de Ferro and Fosfobox, and the super parties at Fundição Progresso (an old 19th-century stove factory), were the forerunners of the electronic wave that launched in the late 1990s and took hold in the 2000s. Among the founders of this music scene were DJs like Maurício Lopes, Felipe Venâncio, Nepal, Gustavo Tatá and the legendary José Roberto Mahr, all of whom still command a loyal following in the city.

Sadly, Rio no longer has a dedicated underground electronic music club. Nonetheless, DJs and clubbers roam around the city, finding and creating parties everywhere from seaside kiosks in São Conrado, Barra and Ipanema, to unusual places downtown, such as the Gamboa and Lapa districts. Lapa, a district full of historic buildings and a trademark 19th-century aqueduct, is a particular hotspot for all kinds of music and entertainment.

The itinerant party Rara is the most famous of the nomadic parties, rocking cariocas (the locals' name for themselves, and also the name of a dance and style of music) with a hearty diet of house music, the city's favourite electronic rhythm. Rio, like Brazil itself, is a musical melting pot where electronic sounds mix with funk carioca as easily as cachaça mixes with brown sugar, ice and lime.

Getting around Rio involves walking or using the subway and the plentiful taxis. Bus routes tend to swing through some of the more deprived favelas and can be a favourite with pickpockets, so are best avoided by the less hardy traveller.

FAU, a rave party in the centre of Rio

DJS / LABEL

Flo Massé
The Franco-Brazilian DJ and drummer Flo is at the head of the itinerant parties Pulso, 4 Finest Ears and Íntima, and has been setting fire to Rio's dancefloors for some years now. Her sets are full of French Touch references and mix house, acid, breaks, minimal and techno.

Rodrigo Facchinetti
DJ and producer Rodrigo Facchinetti is passionate about vinyl culture. His musical research combines the tradition of Brazilian music with current electronic tracks, the result of his relentless search for records in New York and Brazil. His sets are full of international influences, which he blends with revisited Brazilian rhythms to create a solar and organic groove.

Cocada Music
Cocada is a traditional Brazilian delicacy made from grated coconut and sugar, and it is this sweet flavour that producer and record label dealer Leo Janeiro imprints on Cocada Music's releases. "We want to give the world the opportunity to taste the powerful delights that are being produced in Latin America", says the label's bio. Cocada Music is distributed by Get Physical and has released albums featuring Ricardo Villalobos, Jimpster, L_cio and the duo Nu Azeite (Fábio Santanna and Bernardo Campos).

EVENTS

Festival de Ativação Urbana / Urban Activation Festival (FAU)
FAU is a rave party in the historic centre of Rio de Janeiro, in the new Porto Art District between the neighbourhoods of Santo Cristo and Gamboa. The party attracts crowds of up to 2,000 people and is the most inclusive event in town, with all genders and sexual orientations coming together to party on the street. House music is joined by a splash of techno and electronic Brazilian sounds from the skilled hands and hearts of the best DJs in Rio.

Rara
The wandering party Rara has been active since 2015 and is unanimous among carioca clubbers as the most important party on the electronic circuit. DJs Filipe Raposo and Bernardo Campos are in charge of transforming iconic locations in Rio, such as Morro da Urca (next to the Sugar Loaf), Casa França-Brasil in the historic centre, and the middle of the forest in Alto da Boa Vista. The soundtrack is made up of electro, house and techno.

SAO PAULO

From the aisles of a mini-market to the high-tech dancefloor of D-Edge, welcome to Brazil's electronic music capital

Brazil's richest, most cosmopolitan and populous South American city is also the centre of its electronic music scene. With its myriad connections through the Brazilian diaspora and the melting pot of African, European and Asian influences, São Paulo saw an explosion of discotheques, punk and post-punk rock in the music circuit in the 1980s, with the electronic wave taking its first steps here. Club kids, DJs, ecstasy, mixing, techno and house entered the vocabulary of the city's nightlife in the early '90s, and the big turning point came with the afterhours Hell's Club in 1994, which brought Laurent Garnier and Moby to play on Sunday mornings. A succession of festivals, clubs, raves and local DJs followed – notably Marky, Mau Mau, Renato Lopes and Renato Cohen – and the arrival of the futuristic D-Edge, in 2003.

All these years on, D-Edge still has the best sound system and the most glamorous line-ups, but itinerant parties throughout São Paulo testify to the health of the scene. Events take place in all kinds of unusual places: old squares, derelict buildings, warehouses, even in a minimarket where you can dance between food aisles (Mercado Do Lasanha). Look out for Cashu's (Carol Schutzer) Mamba Negra techno party, which transforms different warehouses and even parking lots into dancefloors. Paribar is a club space based around an old restaurant and bar from the 1940s and a square behind the municipal library downtown, where it hosts parties in the late afternoons featuring local DJs like Janaina Nas. Fabriketa, a dusty, gutted factory complex, has welcomed everyone from Avalon Emerson to Michael Bibi and Tiga, and even hosted an outpost of Dekmantel. The Brazilian edition of Time Warp also happens in São Paulo with a line-up – Kølsch, Sven Vath, Four Tet – to rival any other electronic festival on the planet.

São Paulo's techno institution, D-Edge

São Paulo has options for all tastes and budgets. The locals dress down for dancing, though they do love to accessorise with a few eccentricities, from giant sunglasses to the still near ubiquitous trucker cap. Clubs don't get going before midnight. The gay scene is a big driver of electronic music in the city, and one of the current highlights is the Brutus party, where hits from the past and new house and techno fill Casa da Luz, an 18th-century mansion in the most decadent area of downtown São Paulo. In fact, parties that celebrate diversity have very much become a feature in recent years. More and more women and transgender artists are commanding the sound as DJs and performers, substantially changing the integration between all genders and races on the dancefloor.

DJ Mau Mau at DGTL Festival

DJS / LABEL

DJ Marky
Perhaps the most famous and influential drum'n'bass DJ from outside the UK, Marky has built a worldwide following since his move to London in 1998 led to a legendary residency at The End, and a golden Essential Mix in 2004 for BBC Radio 1. A global festival favourite who has pioneered his own rich take on the genre with Brazilian, Latin, jazz and acid influences, most of his gigs these days are in Europe, but he remains a legend in his hometown.

ANNA
Though born 75 miles north of the city, in the town of Amparo (where her DJ father owned a club), it was São Paulo's techno scene in the early '00s that shaped Ana Miranda's rise to global stardom. Her first big breakthrough landed on Diynamic in 2016, the eerily restrained 'Odd Concept' with its throat-throbbing bass, driving drums and head-spinning, room-panning melody. The track picked up nods from label boss Solomun, as well as Carl Cox and Joseph Capriati, and caught the attention of audiences and DJs worldwide.

D.O.C Records
Famed for his releases on Kompakt, Brazilian producer Gui Boratto is also the head of D.O.C Records. Its name comes from the expression 'Denominazione di Origine Controllata', used to certify wines, cheeses and other Italian foods. From the music (house and techno) to the cover design, the label's productions are correspondingly refined and melodic, and highlights on the roster include producers L_cio and Elekfantz.

CLUBS

D-Edge
The most international club in Brazil is a black box lit by neon lights and powered by a very high quality sound system, with two floors, a lounge and a terrace. With a real sense of involvement in the global techno scene, D-Edge hosts DJ workshops with Pioneer crossover events, featuring clubs like fabric in London, and guests from locals like Anderson Noise to San Francisco's Adnan Sharif.

Jerome
Despite its slightly odd location next to a cemetery, this small club is one of the coolest in São Paulo. A mixed gay and straight crowd parties on a Friday night to disco and classics, while Saturdays are deeper and techier. Look out for local polymath Manu Vilas's Animal Planet parties on a Sunday, which bristle with dark and hypnotic techno.

⊙ RECORD SHOPS

Dance Division / Show Me Your Case
In the small Dance Division store at Galeria Ouro Fino, a shopping gallery that in the '90s–'00s was the centre of fashion, music and style in the city, you can find everything from classics to new productions in various electronic genres, as well as some rarities of rock, jazz and reggae. For a more curated experience, put yourself in the hands of DJ Mimi at her store Show Me Your Case, a vinyl specialist in techno, house, bossa nova and pearls of Brazilian music.

SANTA CATARINA

In the jungle, the Atlantic jungle, no one sleeps tonight...

Punters capture the sunset at Warung Beach Club

A 10-hour drive from São Paulo, the isolated coast of the Atlantic Forest by the city of Balneário Camboriú is an unlikely location for electronic music. But when a group of friends founded Warung Beach Club here in 2002, everything would change.

Designed along the lines of a Balinese Temple, Warung is one of the most stunning nightclubs in history, and over the course of time it has been put on every DJ's bucket list. It's built around two spaces: a main room with an open end, where the sun rises after a night of raving, and an outside terrace with a view across the Atlantic. "There is literally nothing," reckons DJ Lauren Lane, "like experiencing a sunrise set in the garden at Warung, in-between the beautiful beach and the green Atlantic Forest."

While the indoors has an intense, hands-in-the air big room energy, ideal for the techno of acts like Marco Carola, the Garden is a more spiritual, housey affair. Since Warung opened, other clubs and events have followed in the area, attracting more melodic and progressive rhythms. With the likes of Hernan Cattaneo, Sasha, Timo Maas and more, the area is starting to be known as the 'Brazilian Ibiza'.

The capital of the state, Florianopolis, on the island of Santa Catarina, has a small electronic scene, with beach parties like Trip to Deep, where house music and chilled techno reign.

In nearby Blumenau, known as 'the most German city in Brazil', hard techno party the Phobia Project welcomes a crowd in black leather and S&M gear while performers juggle fire.

The popularity of Warung and the new club industry has even started to affect the local infrastructure; formerly only approachable by fleets of little boats, the club now has its own bridge. With a majority Brazilian crowd and parties at least once a month, Warung is the standard-bearer for this unlikely and remote outpost of global club culture.

DJS / LABEL

BLANCAh
Warung resident BLANCAh (Patricia Laus Mattos) releases her dark and quirky productions on the British label Renaissance and Berlin's Steyoyoke. Besides touring the world, she's a headline essential for festivals across the region.

Danee
Balneario Camboriu native Danee is one of the most popular of DJs at seaside parties in Santa Catarina due to his very technical sets and versatile explorations of house and techno. He is part of the artistic-musical collective Lapso, which also promotes small electronic parties.

Totoyov Music
A techno and variants label that has already released over 50 digital works and a special series on vinyl, Toyotov is commanded by producer Arthus, who swapped Brasília for Balneário Camboriú and has been investing in new names in the Brazilian and international electronic scene, with remixes signed by producers from labels such as Get Physical, 8bit and Moon Harbour.

CLUBS

Surreal Art Park
The newest venture by DJ Renato Ratier, founder of D-Edge in São Paulo, is located in a large green area with a lake and three circus tents that act as dancefloors of different musical styles. The mood is a fun electronic picnic in a garde /outdoor art gallery, and the park also hosts Brazil's version of BPM festival with the likes of Carl Craig, Joris Voorn and Dubfire.

O RECORD SHOP

Acaiá Café
A mix of café, record store and small art gallery, Acaiá Café is a meeting point for young DJs and creatives in Balneário Camboriú. At night, there are intimate performances by musicians and local DJs. Second-hand Brazilian and international rarities are the strong point of the shop, in addition to good coffee and beer.

BUENOS AIRES

After facing an existential threat in 2016, the scene in Argentina's capital is bouncing back stronger than ever

Joris Voon performs at a *Mixmag* event at Palacio Alsina

The Argentine electronic scene harks back to the late 1980s and early 1990s with the pioneering Radio Energy raves, DJs like Diego Ro-K, Carlos Alfonsín, Javier Zuker, Javier Bússola, Aldo Haydar and Pfirter, and later, Hernán Cattáneo's influential residency at Clubland. But it was the visit of the Love Parade festival in 1999 and 2000, named 'Buenos Aires Energy Parade', that really demonstrated that this city of tango and so many other Latin styles also had a thirst for electronic music.

On 21 September 2000, nearly 200,000 people gathered in the Bosque de Palermo park under the slogan: "LOVE, PEACE AND DANCE", to witness headliner and local legend Dero blast out the hard house and techno. Soon after, more and more international festival brands would start to touch down in BA, notably English rave-up Creamfields, whose first non-UK event was held in Buenos Aires in 2001 – a bold move given that Argentina's famously mercurial economy was then in the grip of a brutal crisis.

But Creamfields would thrive, returning for seven more years in succession and establishing BA as a city that would attract the likes of Time Warp, Sonar and MUTEK alongside home-grown events. While Creamfields and others brought the world's biggest names to Argentina, BA DJs like Cattáneo, Martin

Garcia, Deep Mariano, Jay West, Barem and Zuker would all help shape the sound of the city. Whether working in progressive house or minimal techno, they always somehow retained an aura of contemporary-yet-Latin elegance, like the city itself.

Then, tragedy. After five apparent drug deaths at Time Warp in 2016, the local organisers were arrested, electronic music festivals were completely banned from the city and there was even an attempt by the city's Mayor to shut down clubs, too. After stricter laws on drug use and safety regulations, festivals in Buenos Aires started up again in 2017. Locations like the Mandarine Park near Palermo are where FISHER, Amelie Lens and Dixon have all recently played large outdoor shows. Barcelona/Lisbon biggie Primavera Sound debuted in the Parque De los Niños, another riverside green spot, in 2022.

And while there are plenty of bustling Barrios full of great bars, food and restaurants (La Cañitas, Recoleta and Puerto Madero, for example), it's Palermo where the club scene mainly resides. Crobar, right next to Bosque De Palermo, is the biggest, a warehouse style venue under brick arches that holds around 2,000 people. Relatively expensive for entry and drinks, Crobar books DJs like Loco Dice and Len Faki on big nights. Nearby, archway restaurant/outdoor space Avant Garten is a good spot for midweek record label showcases with online vinyl platform Cyberwax. At the other end of Palermo's Ave Juan B. Justo is the Under Club, which is not, as the name might suggest, a Lynx-smelling haven for 16-year-old ravers, but a boxy space about half the size of Crobar that had the first Funktion-One system in the city. The Under Club has an on-the-pulse booking policy that has lately included everyone from VTSS to I Hate Models. The very nearby Niceto is a similarly angular 1,500-cap live music venue that also hosts some interesting electronic events, with guests like Japanese DJ Masda of Cabaret Recordings or the warehouse techno of Dutchman Dimi Angélis. Clubs here don't really get going till 2am and finish at 6am, and don't assume most people will speak English – a little Spanish or even Italian can come in very handy.

DJS / LABEL

Barem
Swept up in the minimal wave of the mid '00s, Mauricio Barembuem would become a key part of the Minus crew, touring the world with Richie Hawtin and co. (and appearing regularly in and alongside their magic cube – you'll want to look it up). He left, amicably, in 2015 to form the less conceptual sounding Fun Records with buddy Alexis Cabrera.

Juana Molina 'Halo'
The daughter of a professional Tango singer, former comedy actress Molina has spent more than two decades constructing her own magical world with experimentalist electronica as her base – a kind of aural version of the Latin American magical realism of author Gabriel García Márquez and director Guillermo del Toro. The acceptable face of folktronica, her dreamy, scuzzy sound with murmured vocals is often utterly bewitching.

Sudbeat
Created by Hernán Cattáneo in 2009 to explore the "hypnotic and subtle side of electronic music" (often in practices where melodic techno and grooving progressive house rub shyly up against each other), Sudbeat has released artists from Amber Long to Eelke Kleijn to Nick Warren.

CLUB

Palacio Alsina
Formerly known as 'Big One', the 2,000-cap Palacio is a spectacular venue reminiscent of Printworks in London – or, indeed, a Victorian prison. Its tiers of balconies overlook a narrow dancefloor, albeit far more elegant thanks to its Art Nouveau cornices and ironwork and with huge projections on the ceiling and walls transforming it into immersive pop art. This is where Mixmag South America regularly brings huge international guests to the city, from Diplo to Joris Voorn.

O RECORD SHOP

AZ Dicos
Veteran local DJs Carlos Alfonsín and Javier Zuker got together in 2021 to fulfil a childhood dream to open their own record store in Villa Crespo. It holds around 15,000 vinyls ranging across rock, pop, acid jazz, funk, and all kinds of electronic music, from house to jungle and even hip-hop.

Solardo behind the decks at Palacio Alsina

MON TEVI DEO

The most chilled-out of all South American capitals has dancefloors packed with aspiring DJs and deep love for all things analogue

A city of parks, trees, beaches and a 14-mile boardwalk along its coastline, by day Montevideo is renowned as the most relaxed of South American capitals. The people here don't like to be rushed, would rather walk than drive, and drugs are not criminalised for personal use. On top of this, the attention to detail and craft required for analogue production and vinyl DJing is prized. Uruguayan law protects books and records against onerous import taxes, which has helped make it the centre of vinyl culture in the continent (though many DJs and producers make frequent trips to Europe to supplement their collections).

But by night it's a different story. Montevideo is a melting pot city where clubs open at midnight and get going even later. The national rhythm is Candombe, a three-drum beat developed by the descendants of freed African slaves. Electronic music gained a foothold in the early 1990s in clubs like X and La Factoría, and gay clubs like Spok and Metrópolis. International artists like Richie Hawtin and Darren Emerson flocked here, inspiring a generation of Uruguayan DJs including Z@p, Kino, DJ Koolt, Emilio, Tania Vulcano, Omar Chibbaro, Nicolas Lutz, Fede Lijtmaer, Nico Etorena and Manuel Jelen. Dancefloors tend to be packed with aspiring DJs, though veterans like Koolt often bemoan the 'brain drain' that sees promising young artists heading to Europe to build a career in places like Berlin or Ibiza.

Today, the main hub for the club scene is Phonotheque, a 500-cap, low-slung space where DJs like Lutz and Koolt play in front of a trippy video projection. A promoter to look out for is Omnia, who've brought names like Patrice Bäumel to warehouse space Complejo Sala Show, while the Budapest Bar, Techsonic Club and Inmigrantes venues host parties like the Berlin-style techno event Mauerfall or showcases from local labels like U're Guay Records. There's a constant rotation of local artists every Saturday through the SOHO club in Punta del Este in the Puerto area, alongside weekly resident DJ Javier Misa. The Soundgarden Festival has an emphasis on progressive house, bringing acts like Nick Warren, Hernán Cattáneoo and Eelke Kleijn to the city in 2019.

The Parque Rodó neighbourhood is home to spots like The Living Bar, a quirky, lo-fi pub where you'll find up-and-coming DJs and live acts, and the chic daytime bar/café La Bicicletta, both good places to find out about the itinerant parties happening weekly across Montevideo's golf clubs, beach bars, outlying fincas and inner city warehouse spaces.

A mainstay on international festival line-ups, Nicolas Lutz goes b2b with Craig Richards at Love International

DJS / LABEL

Nicolas Lutz
A 'DJ's DJ', legendary crate digger and vinyl evangelist, the enigmatic Lutz is an artist in demand everywhere, from festivals like Love International and Houghton, to Fabric and the White Hotel. His occasional mix releases regularly spark a frenzy on track ID resources like The Identification of Music Group.

Lila Tirando A Violet
Releasing on Mexico City's N.A.A.F.I, Tirando fuses the Latin rhythms of dancehall, reggaeton, dembow and bachata with influences including cyberpunk anime, pop anthems and hardcore to create a highly conceptual musical dystopia. Her 2020 Limerencia album was made while she was undergoing treatment for a neurological condition that required her to work for months in dim light.

Saviatek
Built on a foundation of Candombe (and even pre-Colombian sounds like the siku panpipe) but fused with futuristic sounds, Montevideo's Salviatek was founded in 2015 by Uruguayan producers Lechuga Zafiro and Pobvio. Their aim is to draw attention to the inequalities in South American society with challenging, experimental music that showcases regional artists.

O RECORD SHOP

Sebucan Records
A riot of painted cartoon characters on the outside and with a DJ set-up and stacks of old and new electronic vinyl inside, Sebucan Records is one of a handful of record stores in the capital that sell techno, along with Atemporal, Montevideo Second Hand Vinyl store and Stu Discos.

SAN TIAGO

Techno came to Chile to fight facism. Then it stuck around

Ricardo Villalobos holds a flag with the slogan, "Chile Desperto" (meaning "Chile woke up")

Electronic music in Chile was born as a reaction to extremist government policy. As the Pinochet dictatorship of 1973–1990 became more repressive, Chilean political exiles in Germany smuggled vinyl into the country, while people rebelled against the fascist regime and its curfews with raves and illegal parties. Dancing was a rare opportunity for freedom and self-expression.

The legendary Dandy Jack brought the first techno music from Germany at the end of the '80s, sowing the seeds of the Chilean take on the genre together with fellow exiles including Ricardo Villalobos, Cristian Vogel and Chica Paula. The first massive parties began in 1991, at the end of the Pinochet dictatorship, when the Euphoria collective held raves in open-air venues, factories and old buildings. "At that time it was very difficult to hold parties in Santiago," remembers Carlos Latorre D'Ottone aka DJ Zikuta. "But the great difference was made with the Eclipse party". Held in 1994 in the extreme north of the Alacran Peninsula , with icons of the Chilean scene like Ricardo Villalobos and Dandy Jack joined by international pioneers like Stacey Pullen, John Acquaviva, Derrick May and Richie Hawtin, Eclipse marked a milestone in techno culture in the country and laid the foundation of the Chilean-European connection, a mantle taken up especially by Luciano ('The Captain') over the years.

Today, Santiago has one of the most powerful electronic scenes in Latin America, a stopping point for the biggest global festivals: Time Warp, Creamfields, DGTL and Primavera have all touched down here. The minimal, techno and tech house scene has not stopped growing since the nineties, with international guests joined by more and more local DJs and producers, including Felipe Venegas, Alejandro Vivanco and Umho, and female talent like Delphie, Josefina Díaz and Karin von Mühlenbrock.

Most of the clubs and discos are located near the Bellavista neighborhood, where you'll find leading venue La Feria as well as Club Room and Teatro C. Clubs like Subterraneo and Blondie and the Dreambeach festival lean a little more commercial but are worth keeping an eye on. Blondie, one of the oldest nightspots in the town, was the scene of one of the city's most fondly remembered events: when Jeff Mills performed his 'The Exhibionist 2' show there in November 2015 for more than a thousand people.

Outdoor parties like Piknic Électronik are held in different city parks or the Pablo Neruda Amphitheater, home of the Sundeck events, where Villalobos is a regular. Then there's Luciano's Magik Garden Festival, bringing DJs like Loco Dice, Sven Väth, Richie Hawtin, Jamie Jones and Chris Liebing to the Espacio Broadway. Look out for bars that can turn from relaxed and laid-back to intense and buzzing, seemingly at the flip of a switch, like Santo Remedio bar and micro club Mirage Bar Terraza, as well as Studio Mistral at La Feria. Visitors to this hectic city are advised to plan their schedules, arrive early and be organised. Most of the clubs open their doors from 10pmto 5am, and peak around from 2am till close when the main artist takes to the decks.

Rebolledo performs at outdoor party Piknic

○ RECORD SHOP

Groove & Flavor
One of the only places in the city to buy electronic music on vinyl, G&F's selection of new and used discs is found inside the Casa Sonido music academy (founded by local artists and DJs and offering courses on production) near the banks of the Mapocho on Pérez Valenzuela, where the crew also hold regular parties.

Ricardo Villalobos

Among the most innovative yet best loved DJ/producers in the history of techno, Villalobos' offbeat take on the genre, his relentless perfectionism when it comes to sound quality, and his probably exaggerated reputation for hedonism were as much a part of the genre's post-millennial renaissance as his unique, epoch-defining tracks like 'Easy Lee' and 'Dexter'. Having moved to Germany with his family at the age of three to flee the dictatorship, he's a legend in Chile and an instant sell-out headliner from London's fabric to Ibiza's DC10.

Dinky

Alejandra Del Pilar Iglesias Rivera (her sister gave the slightly more efficient nickname when she was a baby) is part of Chile's second generation of techno artists, born and raised in Santiago before setting out for Berlin in 2003. Her 2005 release, 'Acid In My Fridge' on Sven Väth's label Cocoon, catapulted her to fame, and her residency at Panorama Bar (initiated in 2004) endures to this day.

Drumma Records

Founded by Felipe Venegas in 2011, Drumma's mission is to release strong and organic underground tracks with "meaningful rhythms" that are immediately dancefloor-ready. Artists on the roster include Julian Perez, Villalobos, Umho, Jorge Savoretti and Bendejo.

La Feria

Now powered by clean energy (via solar panels on the roof) La Feria has been the crucible of Chile's club scene for more than 20 years despite only holding 300 people. Playing a key role in the story of Villalobos and Luciano, this stylish red-lit tunnel with a carefully engineered Funktion-One system has hosted everyone from Paco Osuna to Lauren Lo Sung and Pan-Pot.

Time Warp Chile

Debuting in 2022 at the mammoth Espacio Riesco Expo Centre, a giant space-age building that looks exactly like a Stormtrooper base on the ice world of Hoth, the Mannheim megarave boasted a line-up that took in Seth Troxler, Charlotte de Witte and Maceo Plex, alongside local heroes Umho and Alejandro Vivanco.

The legendary Dandy Jack, who first brought techno music to Chile from Germany in the 1980s

77

Santiago's Blondie Club, one of the oldest nightlife spots in the city

Lisboa

Manchester

London

Beograd

Chapter 3

EUROPE

Amsterdam

Beograd

Lisboa

Milano

Berlin

London

Manchester

København

Berlin

Amsterdam

Milano

København

Beog

Amsterdam

LONDON

From Afro House to Adonis, drum'n'bass to DIY club crews, railway arches to repair shops, London's club scene is irrepressible

The birthplace of the Second Summer of Love, drum'n'bass, dubstep (with a nod to satellite town Croydon), and countless other genres and innovations in club culture, as well as being home to labels from Hyperdub to Defected, London's nightlife is like bubbles in wallpaper. When redevelopment or gentrification pushes down on the scene in one area, other venues, nights and parties will always find somewhere else to pop up.

Until 2022, the city's flagship (certainly in terms of size, firepower and spectacle) was Printworks. Former home of the gargantuan presses for the likes of the *Daily Mail* and *Evening Standard* newspapers, this 5,000-cap space was so spectacular that it formed the backdrop for blockbuster movies. A day or night spent at Printworks was like being in an indoor festival, while the main room, which has hosted everyone from Flying Lotus to Solomun to Marco Carola, is one of the most dazzling immersions in dance music. Creative director Simeon Aldred confesses that "our lighting budget at Printworks on one night would do lighting for a whole year at smaller clubs." The Dockyards, a new venue from the same team, will hope to fill the rather large void in the capital's club scene.

But London's musical palette has something for every taste, from avant-garde electronica at Cafe OTO, huge drum'n'bass events (such as Andy C playing Wembley's mammoth SSE Arena,

Hospitality at Studio 338, or Metalheadz at E1), to big scale tech house at Tobacco Dock with DJs like Hot Since 82 or Jamie Jones. You can find the hottest in house and techno at XOYO, or community based clubs nurturing new sounds and fledgeling promoters at FOLD, Corsica Studios, or even MOT Unit 18, a converted auto workshop in Bermondsey.

Meanwhile, a dynamic spectrum of DIY collectives provide continual renewal, from those fusing the sounds of London's diaspora (like the Afro House Motherland and South Asian crew No ID) to carving out their own crowd, like the queer facing drum'n'bass night Unorthodox Event, or Steam Down's remarkable live jazz fusion parties. Afterparties and Sunday parties like the mysterious Paravibe keep the diehards raving until Monday morning. Kurupt FM and others have ensured that the sound of UKG will never die, while actual real radio stations Fuse, Rinse, Reprazent and NTS offer anyone, anywhere the chase to dial in and take the musical pulse of the city.

Being criss-crossed by Victorian railways means a supply of stunning arch venues like live/club/art space Village Underground or The Steel Yard. London's revitalised gay scene, revolving around the East End and venues like colourful and friendly bar/club Dalston Superstore, has launched collectives including Horse Meat Disco and Adonis to global acclaim and festival takeovers. In the summer, dozens of festivals including Field Day, Gala, Lovebox and Junction 2 take over green spaces in every corner of the city.

Some think of London as a collection of villages: neighbourhoods like Hackney Wick and Dalston in the east, or Peckham and Brixton in the south, offer a self-contained night out from the evening meal to the next morning at venues like the newly opened Night Tales and Colour Factory (Hackney), Phonox or the Jamm (Brixton), or TOLA in Peckham. But getting around is cheap and easy thanks to the night tube or, for those who enjoy a human safari vibe on their nocturnal journey, the frequent night buses. Nearly forgot: London is home to the Mixmag Lab, live-streaming the world's best DJs and held every Friday at our office.

The crowd at Printworks, London's flagship venue until its closure in 2022

Andrew Weatherall preparing for a set in Paris

Hyperdub's 5th Birthday at Corsica Studios

DJS / LABEL

Andrew Weatherall

One of the UK's original must-see DJs, Weatherall turned his back on superstar DJ culture when it was in its infancy. Though his work on albums such as Primal Scream's *Screamdelica* made him one of the most in-demand producers on the planet, he favoured an authentic, underground approach to the craft. His *raison d'être* (defined on his body by a tattoo saying, "fail we may, sail we must"), his peerless DJing and his myriad productions under names including Sabres Of Paradise and with Two Lone Swordsmen served as an inspiration to artists and clubbers around the globe, and the reaction to his death in 2020 showed just how beloved Lord Sabre had become.

Jaguar

Former *Mixmag* alumni Jaguar has become a champion for the power of club culture to pioneer cultural change with her podcast *Utopia Talks* (interviewing the likes of Fat Tony on sobriety and addiction, Sama' Abdulhadi on DJing in Palestine, and Fabio on the whitewashing of electronic music). She also DJs around the world, hosting the International Music Summit in Ibiza her Utopia events at festivals and club spaces, and her weekly BBC Radio 1 show.

Ninja Tune

Founded in 1990 by pioneering duo Coldcut, who released both the first UK hip-hop album and one of the greatest mix compilations in history back in the day, sometimes it seems like Ninja Tune has a monopoly on electronic artists working in the sweet spot where the dancefloor meets the art of recording. Even just considering the years since 2015, they've helped artists expand their vision to create astonishing LPs, singles, and, indeed, careers, from Bicep to Bonobo, Marie Davidson to Machinedrum, Park Hye Jin to Jayda G and many more. A national treasure.

CLUB / EVENT

Corsica Studios

A favourite venue for everyone from Helena Hauff to Hyperdub Records, and home of nights including Peach Party, Origins, Rhythm Section and the off-the wall TranceParty, Corsica's rough-round-the-edges charms and booming sound system are second only to its impeccable programming. A club that has thrived by putting itself at the centre of the local arts and creative community, it's been a template for scores of others seeking to do the same in the capital.

Junction 2 festival, situated under the imposing concrete structure of the M4 motorway

Junction 2
Originally held under a motorway overpass in London's Boston Manor Park, Junction 2 debuted in 2016 with artists including Dixon, Carl Craig and Nina Kraviz. The festival broke the internet in 2018 when Adam Beyer and Carl Cox played b2b in a live-streamed set, and in 2022 it moved temporarily to Trent Park with a line-up that ranged from Mind Against to Maribou State.

○ RECORD SHOP

Phonica
Soho's Phonica has been an incubator for several counter-hands turned world-renowned DJs, and hosted hundreds of in-store sessions from everyone from Four Tet and Peggy Gou to Leon Vynehall. They launched their own record label in 2008.

FABRIC

It's hard to believe now, but when fabric opened in a former Victorian cold storage building opposite Smithfield meat market in 1999, it was overshadowed by the hype around another club launch in London. So big was the hubbub around the ill-fated Home, launched in tourist hotspot Leicester Square with a red carpet of celebrities and a hubristic mission to "save London's clubland", that the team behind fabric actually delayed their own opening – a decision that came too late for their first advert in *Mixmag*, its phantom DJ line-ups surely now a collector's edition.

But like so much of fabric's history, it proved a master stroke. This was a venue that took the art of clubbing seriously, well before the influence of places like Berlin turned disk jockeys into 'artists'. The sound system, the sprung wooden dancefloor, and the experience for clubbers and DJs alike were always far more important than empty hype. fabric would help define the renegade, melting pot sound of the city, championing hip-hop and breaks with residents such as Scratch Perverts and drum'n'bass to grime (particularly at nights helmed by Rinse FM) and later innovations in bass music on Friday nights at fabriclive.

Building Saturday nights around uncompromising but always forward-looking residents Craig Richards and Terry Francis gave the club a distinct identity and made it a global bellwether for house and techno, while their careful and innovative guest curation broke new talents, including Seth Troxler (and even helped DJs who were pushing new sounds, like Ricardo Villalobos, find a floor that was open, trusting, and hugely influential). fabric became one of a handful of clubs that every DJ who played there, from any part of the world, would add to their bio – a rite of passage and a seal of approval. And you can read the discography of fabric's mix series like a history of global electronic music, from that first, stone-cold classic James Lavelle fabriclive 01 mix (taking in Green Velvet, DJ Shadow and even Smokey Robinson) into recent instalments from a new generation, like Sherelle's adventures in 160bpm or TSHA. Their 24-hour birthday events, often overseen by Villalobos, brought the spirit of marathon Berlin style clubbing to London for the first time.

Then the music stopped. When two young men, Ryan Browne and Jack Crossley, died in the vicinity of the club after taking ecstasy in the summer of 2016, the Met police asked the local council to revoke the licence. The

A shuttered fabric, following its closure in 2016

order to shut the doors came on 7 September. Up until that point, clubs had come and gone in London. Home itself had shut down in 2001, after a long and attritional battle with police and their own council. Venues including The End, Turnmills, Plastic People, the Cross, all much loved in their own way, had closed in the previous 10 years, under pressure from redevelopment, gentrification and licensing authorities. There had been deep regret, but an acceptance that this was the nature of things in the fast moving city.

But with the closure of fabric, the electronic music community – not just in the city but around the world – decided a line had been crossed. DJs and artists, clubbers old and young, fellow promoters and venue owners, the

media, the Night Time Industries Association and even the Mayor of London rallied around the club, and a campaign was launched to save it. More than £300,000 was raised for a legal appeal, with contributors ranging from clubbers chipping in a fiver to superstar DJs and actors pledging much more. 160,000 people signed a petition. The famous birthday party was turned into a fundraising event and split over two venues elsewhere in the city, with Ben UFO, Ricardo Villalobos, Seth Troxler, Joy Orbison and Ben Klock all turning out to play.

The campaign culminated in an emotional, marathon appeal at Islington Council Town Hall on 21 November 2016 , followed live on social media across the planet. The verdict: fabric would be allowed to reopen. There would be stringent, even Draconian, procedures and searches upon entry, but the music would start again. The experience demonstrated just how powerful club culture could be when united. How a venue playing music could come to represent the heartbeat of the city, and have touched so many lives over time. The fundraising and organisational template that the campaign developed would help secure the future of clubs across the world when lockdown hit in 2020. Recently reopened yet again, with a refurb that has injected new blood into the line-ups and stripped back the venue to reveal more of its industrial past, fabric remains a symbol and an inspiration for club culture in London – and beyond.

MAN CHE STER

From the epic Warehouse Project to the innovative White Hotel, Manchester's scene still flourishes, an important resistance to the city's ongoing gentrification

In recent years, two key locations have shaped Manchester's club culture. One is the Warehouse Project, now in its second location in a vast former train factory. This is clubbing as spectacle – epic vistas, epic sound, 10,000 people across three rooms. There's the main Depot room, a cavernous industrial space of tall pillars and lighting that recalls fabric's room one; Concourse is an intimate, '90s style club space with the DJ booth at ground level, and Archive a narrow tunnel fitted with a J-Series sound system from d&b audiotechnik. "It meets somewhere in the middle of a club and an illegal rave," says DJ Sherelle. "It's festival-sized but with a home-grown edge." Since launching in 2006, WHP paved the way for seasonal 'event clubbing' programs in vast reclaimed industrial spaces from Printworks in London to Motion in Bristol. Constantly evolving, perhaps the most thrilling nights are those when an artist or label – Four Tet, say, or Jamie xx – takes over the entire curation of the venue, setting out their vision on the largest of all canvasses.

At the other pole is The White Hotel. Named after D. M. Thomas's 1981 erotic novel, the former car repair shop was transformed in 2015 into a warehouse space split into two rooms, its concrete dancefloor under constant surveillance from a pair of decapitated mannequin heads perched atop a high ledge. Created and curated by a team of multidisciplinary creatives, White Hotel is a space for artistic experimentation in all its forms."You don't know whether you're coming into a cinema, a club, a boozer or a brothel," says author and filmmaker Austin Collings, a key member of the team. The White Hotel is backed up by a music program that ranges across the international underground from Kode9 to Helena Hauff, while a keen eye for talent has helped locals from Annabel Fraser to Space Afrika make their breakthrough. WH makes the most of Salford's relaxed licensing laws (compared to the rest of the city) with a 7am close, and an event called Studio 54½hrs recently saw the hotel open for 54 solid hours and 30 minutes across a weekend.

What both venues have in common is an ambitious vision for Manchester's club scene to push the envelope, whether that's in scale or cultural contribution. Perhaps it can be traced back to entrepreneur and visionary

The White Hotel, a former car repair shop situated in the shadow of a ruined tower, was transformed into a venue in 2015

Tony Wilson, a driving force behind Factory Records and the Hacienda, but its legacy can be seen everywhere, from the efforts of his son Oli to launch an electronic music festival in the city or Moston rapper Aitch's creation of NQ House, a studio complex in a converted residence designed to offer opportunities for young creatives.

Between these two poles are a raft of venues and parties still holding out against the city's relentless ongoing makeover into a Ballardian dormitory of apartment complexes and 'student living': the 29-year-strong Joshua Brooks club, SOUP in the Northern Quarter, and Hidden and Sounds From The Other City in Salford. Look out for events by Homoelectric, an underground collective who've almost single-handedly turned the queer clubbing scene in the city from cheese fest to cutting edge.

A compact city, nights out in Manchester can be spontaneous and varied thanks to low entry prices and short distances between venues. SOUP aside, the tourist magnet of the Northern Quarter is shunned by most locals in favour of Ancoats and Salford these days. One of Manchester's standout qualities is the way club culture is open to all ages, thanks to the efforts of figures like Luke Unabomber to make older clubbers feel welcome: "The acid house generation has grown up a bit," says Luke, "but they still want to go out and listen to good music in a chilled-out environment." The Refuge and Escape to Freight Island in particular pride themselves on a broad age demographic without compromising the experience or the music.

...vast spectacle of epic vistas, epic sound and 10,000 people across three rooms.

Manchester's finest, DJ Paulette

DJS / PRODUCER / LABEL

DJ Paulette
The first female resident of the Hacienda, Paulette's two-decade career has seen her bring her bass heavy vocal house sound everywhere from Ibiza to Paris. The affection towards her in the city was perhaps best demonstrated by the 6,000 visitors to an exhibition dedicated to her life at Manchester's Lowry Gallery.

The Unabombers
Stalwarts of the Manchester scene since they started pioneering club night Electric Chair back in 1995, Luke Cowdrey and Justin Crawford and have been part of shaping club culture in the city with their involvement in venues such as The Refuge, Escape to Freight Island and The Warehouse Project. "It's rooted in people's need to escape monotone life in a black and white town," says Luke. "When things were grey, music was a fundamental part of that."

Anz
Building on her monthly NTS radio show, London-born Anz has become a Manchester breakthrough star thanks to sets that she describes as "a testament to my indecisiveness": anything from garage, UK funky, breakbeat, hardcore and jungle to footwork, gqom, baile

London-born Anz has become a Manchester breakthrough star

…unk, Baltimore club and Afrobeats, "with some liberal pitch-fader use." Her own production output is prolific: Anz runs label OTM and co-hosts night 'A Party Called' across the city and beyond.

Skam Records
Started by local DJ Andy Maddocks and representing Manchester since 1990, Skam Records has consistently championed UK talent from the leftfield – notably Autechre from nearby Rochdale and Scottish downtempo analogue duo Boards of Canada. The label continues to showcase talent with the recent release of local composer,DJ and producer Afrodeutsche's debut LP.

CLUB / EVENT

SOUP
An intimate, 200-cap basement venue below a bar and highly rated canteen, SOUP specialises in supporting local live talent and giving a home to some of the city's most musically forward-thinking LGBTQ+ nights, alongside occasional visits by international names like Objekt and Mosca.

Parklife
The biggest inner city festival in the UK, Parklife occupies Heaton Park for two days every June, boasting eight stages and more than 80,000 ravers per day. The overwhelmingly electronic line-up boasts huge headliners from Carl Cox and Bicep to 50 Cent and Tyler, the Creator, with dedicated drum'n'bass, house and techno arenas.

The aftermath of The Warehouse Project

○ RECORD SHOP

Eastern Bloc Records
Established in 1985, Eastern Bloc has always been more than just a repository of electronic music on vinyl. It's also an events space, café and bar that regularly hosts showcases from visiting and local DJs, including big name pre-shows from the mezzanine. Staff pride themselves on being friendly and accessible – and on their horizon-broadening suggestions.

Parklife, the biggest inner-city festival in the UK

THE HACIENDA

One thing that the members of Manchester band New Order were great at doing was spending money. Everyone knows the story about the sleeve design for the 12in mega hit 'Blue Monday' being so expensive to produce that the band lost money for every copy they sold, but it was with the Hacienda that the band truly excelled themselves. In 1982, fresh from chart success with 'Temptation' and 'Blue Monday' (and inspired by New York's blossoming club scene) they opened a nightclub.

Actually, their vision was even more ambitious: a cultural hub for artists, musicians and creative people. "We wanted to build a place where we'd want to hang out," remembers bassist Peter Hook. If that sounds like a concept people are still pitching to investors 40 years later, maybe that was the problem. The Hacienda was light years ahead of its time.

Resident DJ Greg Wilson started laying a foundation with his Friday night of funk and electro in 1983, one of the first to bring the city's Black and white communities to the same dancefloor, and Madonna made one of her first live appearances in the UK at the club a year later. But it wasn't until the nationwide acid house explosion in 1987, and Graeme Park and Mike Pickering's NUDE night, that the club stopped making a loss every week.

Popularity brought its own problems. Some practicalities had been surrendered to aesthetics. "Nobody had considered that for a club licensed to hold 1,200 people we'd need more than four toilets for the men and eight for the girls," remembers Hooky. "We let in 2,000 people, so the bogs overflowed all the time and everyone in the basement walked around ankle-deep in piss and shit. Quite horrible, but it became a standing joke. 'Hacienda trousers', we called it." Despite that, NUDE, and Balearic night Hot, inspired the Madchester music scene, which saw indie bands like the Happy Mondays and The Stone Roses fuse their guitar sound with dance production and copious ecstasy consumption. The Hacienda's innovative nights dispelled the idea that indie and electronic music had to stay in their own lanes, bringing electronic producers like Andrew Weatherall and Paul Oakenfold into the mainstream music industry, and introducing the concept that a nightclub could be as treasured a part of a city's identity as any museum, art gallery or cathedral. The club itself would become legend. Now it's been replaced by apartments (named after the club, naturally), but the best of it endures thanks to the FAC 51 The Hacienda parties that tour the UK and beyond.

Dancing at the Hacienda in 1990

GLASGOW

SLAM at Riverside Festival

Home to scene-leading figures such as Slam and Optimo and some of the most up-for-it crowds on the planet

The defining characteristics of Glasgow's club scene are loyalty and longevity. The focal point of the city's club culture remains the legendary Sub Club, 35 years young with the same Saturday night residency, Harri and Domenic's Subculture, still in place.

Many of the figures and promoters still leading the charge; Pressure, Optimo, STREETrave, and Colours all date back to when acid house first reached the city and continue to operate. But there's also constant renewal. The vast SWG3 club has filled the void left by the much-lamented closure of Arches in 2015, metastasising somehow from an unlicensed rave-up in a neglected part of town to a club/hub spread over eight different spaces, including a giant main space and an outdoor courtyard. June's Riverside festival, held by the Clyde quays (once the engine room of empire), launched a few years ago and celebrates local talent alongside carefully curated international guests from Carl Cox to Charlotte de Witte.

As in many post-industrial cities, techno has long been the backbone of the scene, but there are more eclectic spaces to be found, from the Berkeley Suite, an art-deco-styled basement where disco and house reign, to the small-but-perfectly formed La Cheetah, where Nightwave pushes the boundaries with her residency. Club 69, found in the basement of a curry house in satellite city Paisley, was the unlikely key staging ground for label and promoter LuckyMe's post-dubstep explorations with the likes of Hudson Mohawke and Numbers's prolific eclecticism.

Most clubs get up to full intensity early thanks to a pre-refreshed crowd and a standard closing time of 3am. The city's compact centre means that nothing is too far away, which makes visits to a couple of clubs in a night more than feasible. The West End and the Merchant City are the best neighbourhoods for bars, and if the area around Central Station becomes a little post-apocalyptic at chucking out time (complete with feral bands squabbling over scarce resources like fish suppers and black taxis), that's more than made up for by a recklessly inclusive afterparty scene and a welcoming, friendly vibe among the locals towards visitors and tourists. A chant of "WAN MORE TUNE" remains the polite form of appreciation if the closing DJ has smashed it.

Denis Sulta at Riverside Festival

Nightwave
Slovenian-born renaissance woman Nightwave is one of the most pioneering figures in the city's recent scene. From her La Cheetah residency, grounded in Detroit techno, electro, acid, Chicago house and old rave nostalgia, to her carefully curated imprint Heka Trax, to her tireless work on promoting equality in the music industry, she's a key figure in Glasgow's continuing evolution.

Denis Sulta
The peroxide-haired rave sprite has become an international headliner thanks to his exquisitely constructed, constantly imaginative festival sets and the creative chaos of his club shows. A regular at Riverside Festival, for sheer DJ showmanship backed with deep musical knowledge, few come close.

SOMA
The city's original techno titans SLAM haven't just driven the genre in the city since the '80s with their Pressure party, and created one of the most raucous festival experiences on the planet with the 'Slam Tent' at the first T In the Park, and latterly TRNSMT festival. Stuart McMillan and Orde Meikle's incredible and relentlessly consistent label, SOMA, was responsible for Daft Punk's first release (the 'New Wave' EP), and standards are as high to this day.

CLUBS / EVENT

La Cheetah
Despite only holding 200 people, La Cheetah has built relationships with some of the most exciting talents around: for its 10th anniversary in 2019, Objekt, Shanti Celeste and Avalon Emerson each hosted a four-part series of parties. The recent opening of slightly bigger sister venue Room 2 has only broadened the canvas.

Sub Club
This low-ceilinged, compact gem of a club has an international reputation that's based on its music, crowd and atmosphere, and completely out of proportion with its unpretentious decor and 410-person capacity. "The most intense thing I have ever witnessed," is how visiting DJ Ralph Lawson describes the crowd. "They were shouting so loudly I could hardly hear the next track in my headphones to mix."

Platform 18
This yearly street festival, held under some obscure railway bridges in the City's Southside, is Glasgow's equivalent of DC10 – albeit with trains rattling overhead every so often rather than jets. Previous guests include Richie Hawtin, Ben Klock, Jeff Mills, DVS1, Blawan, Kobosil and Amelie Lens.

○ RECORD SHOP

Monorail
Tucked away inside daytime hangout/vegan café Mono, Monorail is an essential stop for record buyers of a more alternative bent, with a focus on overlooked indie-pop and close relationships with local musical aristocracy, from Optimo to Belle and Sebastian.

Honey Dijon behind the decks at SWG3

OPTIMO (ESPACIO)

When Glasgow's JD Twitch started his own club night in 1997, it was in part because he wanted to get away from playing seamlessly mixed house and techno and showcase some of the other music in his collection, from post punk and shoegaze to Afrobeat and ambient. After asking fellow DJ Johnnie Wilkes to join him, their ambition became something more: "a return to the ideals of early '80's New York where lots of different scenes (hip-hop, punk, no wave, disco, gay, straight, art, photography, anything goes) briefly collided into one of the most inspiringly creative moments in the history of art, music and clubbing." At first, locals didn't really know what to make of a Sunday night club where the DJs spent the first few hours playing music to listen rather than dance to. Soon, though, it would build a loyal following and become one of the most important, and influential, nights on the planet.

Optimo was among the first to bring the likes of Soulwax and The Rapture to the UK, along with countless other live acts, old and new, hyped or overlooked. This was one of the first places where guitars met electronic: Franz Ferdinand were born on the dancefloor at Optimo. It was Optimo that influenced the creation of nights like London's Trash and Nag Nag Nag and the mindset of artists as far away geographically as James Murphy's DFA Records in New York. Optimo helped catalyse scenes from electroclash at the turn of the millennium to new rave in the mid '00s.

The duo's DJ sets somehow put disparate genres and tracks together in a context that made musical sense without losing their cathartic fun. Call it 'musical education by stealth'. Most of all, though, Optimo was a space where the many Glaswegians who liked a little bit of art alongside their dancing could express themselves. The club's Halloween parties saw the venue, the attendees, and the DJs transformed according to a different theme each year. They are the stuff of legend, and every electronic artist to come through Glasgow in the past two decades seems to have been influenced in some way, from Eclair Fifi to Calvin Harris.

While the Sub Club weekly residency ended officially in 2010, Johnnie and Twitch's Optimo Record label continues to break new artists and styles. They continue to be in demand as DJs, and occasional events such as the Optimo 20th birthday at SWG3 in 2017 (guests included The Blessed Madonna and Ben UFO) are a reminder of their continuing influence.

JD Twitch and Jonnie Wilkes behind the decks at Love International

DUBLIN

Ireland's resilient club scene may lack larger venues, but this craic is very moreish

Dublin's club scene has been through the wringer a few times. With the Celtic Tiger wounded by the 2008 recession, promoters found it increasingly hard to keep nights and venues running. In 2012, the Pod trio of venues under one roof closed after nearly 20 years, leaving the almost two million people in the greater Dublin area with no big electronic venues. Ironically, the medium term effect on a city that had long depended on overseas bookings to maintain momentum was positive. Collectives, DIY events and afterparties started to boom again (though stars like Krystal Klear and Mano Le Tough still had to move overseas to build their careers).

Things started looking up in terms of venues too, with the opening of Opium, Button Factory, Hangar and District 8 (a cavernous, 1,500-cap space on the ground floor of the Tivoli theatre), before taking a hit again in 2015, when legendary club Twisted Pepper closed. District 8 and Hangar closed in 2018, turning into hotels. Counterintuitive, strict licensing rules don't help, though reform is promised soon.

But the scene in Dublin abides, with organisations like DJ and promoter Sunil Sharpe's Give Us the Night (a collective lobbying group for the city's nightlife) offering efforts to open up more and bigger spaces for electronic events, leadership and collaboration among operators, and cross-communication with other cities across the UK and Europe. "There are a lot of issues," says Sunil, "but we know where we are now, and what we need to do to reset." Sunil points to a wave of exciting new producers, collectives and young promoters coming through alongside previous generations of scene stalwarts, including DJs such as Francois, Aoife Nic Canna and Jon Hussey who've stayed involved since year dot.

The dancefloor at Index, the city's most reliably over-subscribed destination

Perhaps the key to getting the most out of Dublin is not to get sucked into the stag/hen/novelty Guinness top hat mega pub scene of Temple Bar, and be prepared to look beyond the city's tourist-heavy Southside. A compact and attractive place, Dublin is easy to get around despite a neglected transport system – but clubs get full quickly and close strictly at 3am here, so make a plan and stick to it. Perhaps head north across the Liffey to the area bounded by Capel and Abbey Streets to find venues like Yamamori Tengu, a restaurant by day, and Grand Social, a pub, which transform into two of the most interesting little club/live spots by night. Just round the corner is the 300-cap Wigwam, another restaurant with a basement and roof terrace; its programming ranges from techno royalty like Surgeon to long-standing city promoter Bodytonic, exploring the more eclectic sounds of UK acts like Interplanetary Criminal or India Jordan. On the north bank of the Liffey you'll find both The Sound House and Here & Now, home to Index. Back south of the river, look out for Bow Lane and especially Pygmalion, a buzzing hangout during the day with international guests spanning Optimo and John Talabot arriving by night. And on the fringes of Temple Bar you'll find the likes of the industrial, experimental-facing TRAMLINE, Tengu's basement sister venue Izakaya, the recently renovated Button Factory, and Cellar, a reincarnation of U2's former Kitchen venue that showcases up-and-coming local acts in an intimate, supportive space. Not a comedy hat in sight.

EMA (1) performing a Boiler Room set

Krystal Klear
Dublin-born Declan Lennon shot to stardom when his infectious banger 'Neutron Dance' was picked up by Gerd Janson's Running Back label in 2018 and hasn't looked back since. Though based in New York, he is a frequent returnee to his hometown – his month-long residency at Pygmalion in 2018 was a definite event. He actually defined his sound, which struts and weaves through disco, electro, New York house and first-generation British rave within the space of a single track,during a period studying in Manchester and a residency at the legendary Hoya:Hoya, as part of a crew that included Illum Sphere, Lone and Eclair Fifi.

EMA (1)
Lead booker at Tengu, EMA (1) runs workshops for female and nonbinary DJs and producers, helms the Woozy party series and label (dedicated to the intersection of bass, dub and soundsystem culture with club sounds) and is a co-founder of Skin&Blister, which has helped create one of the most inclusive parties in the city. As a DJ, besides her residency at Tengu, she's played everywhere from Griessmühle in Berlin to Fabric in London.

D1 Recordings
Founded in 1994 by Eamonn Doyle, D1 is Ireland's OG techno label, growing out of nights spent in the mid '90s at the Funnel – a 300-capacity venue on Sir John Rogerson's Quay – and afterparties at Eamonn's house at 147 on Parnell Street in Dublin 1, in a five-floor building that would welcome a revolving cast of artists and producers over the years. Their artist roster includes everyone from Fatima Yamaha and DJ Bone to Mark Broom to Donnacha Costello.

○ RECORD SHOP

All City records
A sprawling long-established vinyl paradise with an attached street art supplies division and even a barber shop, ACR has long been key to nurturing Dublin's booming electronic talent, from breaking artists on their in-house labels to owner Olan O'Brien's careful mentorship of young producers, musicians and label owners.

CLUBS

Index
One of Dublin's bigger venues, the new home to long-running house and techno promoters Subject and the crew behind the much missed District 8, is also known confusingly at various times as 39/40 and Here & Now. But nomenclature doesn't matter – thanks to huge and exciting bookings like Helena Hauff, 2manydjs and Hannah Wants, it's become the city's most reliably oversubscribed destination. Buy tickets in advance.

Yamamori Tengu
A key outlet for Dublin's young collectives, bass micro scenes, and LGBTQ+ club crews, this Japanese restaurant-cum-300-cap club space was renovated over lockdown to make it even more dancefloor focused. Look out for nights hosted by promotions like Woozy and Skin&Blister, and guests ranging from Dublin born DJ duo Long Island Sound and local hero Efa O'Neil to New York's DJ Python.

The entrance to Japanese eatery/nightclub, Yamamori Tengu

PARIS

Dive into the techno doughnut as the Paris scene radiates ever outwards

The city that gave the world the French Touch in the '90s and later fuelled the electro boom is once again in the process of reinventing itself. With no real available space to repurpose in the city centre proper– the scene by the Seine now defunct after the much-lamented closure of Batofar and Concrete, and the famous Rex Club having seen better days – there's a definite 'doughnut' motion in effect. The city's biggest club experiences are the wave of huge warehouse events taking place in the suburbs and *banlieues* (giant housing estates) on Paris's outskirts, run by collectives and young promoters continually seeking out new spaces, from 'traditional' industrial warehouse buildings to old schools and sports centres.

"We rent the space, we try to be clean and friendly," explains Sina, who co-founded Subtyl, one of the numerous crews that have emerged from this semi-legal party scene. Many of the Parisian collectives active today – such as La Mamie's, Cracki, Haiku, and Distrikt – follow the same model. "When we started, there was no guest list, no backstage, no DJ guest, just local artists. We created something new, that incited other people to do similar things in their own way", he adds. Their strong support of local artists bred a new generation of underground talent: Voiski, François X, Antigone and more recently KAS:ST, AZF and Molécule all started in these circles.

In 2018, forty Parisian collectives, young and old, gathered to form SOCLE (Syndicat des Organisateurs Culturels Libres et Engagés), a union and support network that lobbies for local authorities to allow and recognise their events.

DJs and dancers at a Subtyl party

Their manifesto reads: "The bubbles of poetry we create in our parties are a necessity in the ever-harsher, normative environment of our everyday lives. Let's work together to preserve them". Unfortunately, where there is money to be made, the unscrupulous often follow. There have been incidents of poorly conceived and even dangerous repurposing of buildings by opportunistic or naive crews, with a lack of facilities, security and aftercare for wide-eyed ravers from the city who find themselves wandering around miles from home in the morning with no idea where they are. One recent scandal concerned the ill-conceived idea of an event in a working refuge for asylum seekers, which turned out just as exploitative and inconsiderate as you'd imagine. Look out for parties by crews like those mentioned above, though, and you'll be fine. These parties have also affected the bpm of the scene, with the new younger warehouse crowd embracing ever harder and faster forms of techno, with a corresponding influence on fashion and design – think shiny plastic, strapping, braces and peroxide.

Back in the city, though, there is still fun to be had. The underbelly of the Pigalle area is as punky and cheerfully trashy as ever. The 9th arrondissement is the place to go if you have money to burn, while the 18th is a little more forgiving on finances. Nights out in Paris tend to spread over a few nights and days, with a healthy and relentless afterparty scene for those willing and able to make friends with the right group on a night out. Luckily, the idea that Parisians are haughty and hostile to anyone who doesn't speak French is a

Dancers at a suburban rave in Paris

O RECORD SHOP

Syncrophone Records
Syncrophone has been an institution among Paris house and techno DJs since its genesis in 2005, thanks to its location right next to the Bastille's Babadoum club, label showcase nights at clubs across the city, and the fact that its management team includes two DJs: Didier Allyne and Blaise. Syncrophone also runs an extensive distribution network for French electronic labels.

François X

A leading light of the new French techno renaissance, and co-founder of the DEMENT3D collective and record label, X's style, honed at his residency at Concrete, rages through forgotten techno gems and '90s acid to the latest forward-thinking sounds. His debut album, *Irregular Passion*, was one of the standout releases of 2018, and he's been in high demand at festivals across Europe, as well as making numerous appearances at Berghain.

Cassie Raptor

A former VJ with a substantial Instagram following, Raptor has earned the hype with industrial techno releases like '1984' on Warrior Records, gigs across Paris, and regular appearances at Europe's leading underground spots, from Berlin's Anomalie Art Club to The Cause in London.

Ed Banger

"I guess we were there at the right time and at the right place. Bringing indie kids, hiphop heads and clubbers together. Unity in diversity. Bringing back fun into nightclubs," says Ed Banger supremo Pedro Winter. Record label Ed Banger led the French electro house revolution that took place around 2006 to 2007 with artists like Mr. Oizo, SebastiAn, Uffie, Feadz, DJ Mehdi and, of course, Justice, setting the precedent for an entire wave of artists.

Le Liebe

This late-opening DJ bar in Montmartre has a split-level interior inspired by Communist-era East Berlin. Fuelled by techno and with an open decks night on Thursdays (ironic since the decks are in a cage), it is somehow far more stylish than that sounds.

La Machine du Moulin Rouge

This four room concert venue in the heart of the Pigalle doesn't just have an air of *fin de siècle* Parisian glamour thanks to a 125-year history of cabaret on the same spot; it also hosts some of Paris's best electronic music, from DJ nights by local collectives or Trax Magazine and Rinse France, to live shows from touring acts like Cut Copy and Giant Swan. Always worth a look at the listings when you're in town.

La Machine du Moulin Rouge

RESPECT AT LE QUEEN

Ground zero for the French Touch (the explosion of house music talent in the 1990s that catapulted the likes of Daft Punk, Cassius, Étienne de Crécy, I:Cube, Air and many more to global stardom), Respect was started in 1996 by Jerome Vigler-Kohler (then a lowly intern at Paris's Radio FG), promoter Fred Agostini and radio presenter David Blot. "A lot of the Parisian DJs were finally getting some recognition," remembers Dimitri from Paris. "But while the UK music press were interested in us, no-one really cared in France. The main problem was that the Parisian clubs didn't want to book any French DJs. The DJs that were filling the clubs were all American, like Carl Craig. These guys noticed this and said, 'that's not right'."

Queen, a gay club with a VIP clientele in Paris's main tourist drag of the Champs-Élysées, had a history in house music; David Guetta had been the former artistic director, bringing names like Little Louie Vega and David Morales to the city. But they had never found a way to fill their tricky Wednesday night. It seemed to make sense to hand over control to the radio stations like FG, Générations and Nova where the new sounds of Paris were starting to coalesce. The pretty much unknown local DJs were enthusiastic, cheap, and there was a definite buzz around them. The first event was scheduled for Wednesday, October 2, 1996. The name, 'Respect', as in 'Respect the DJ', was suggested by local DJ and record store director, Ivan Smagghe.

"The very first booking was Daft Punk [whose debut album *Homework* was still a few months from release]," says Dimitri. "The second was me, and then it must have been Cassius. We all knew each other from hanging out in the same two record stores, so the scene existed before that, but the night created a home for us. Almost all of us were only playing for our friends at small evening things at the time. So even though it wasn't a huge space – it was kind of like a dark box with an 800-person capacity – it was the first time any of us had been booked at a major club."

And within a few weeks, the new party, free to enter, became a focal point for the city's young clubbers. Every Wednesday night, a huge line would form on the Champs-Élysées. An album, *Respect is Burning*, would follow, a showcase of French house that could stand alongside the compilations that defined the sound, such as De Crecy's *Superdiscount* series and *My House in Montmartre*. As Daft Punk exploded and the filtered house sound of Paris started to take over the planet, the club and its DJs were invited to tour the world and spread the vibe. Finally, French electronic music had the respect it deserved.

Daft Punk light up Oxegen festival in Ireland – a far cry from the sweaty, DIY days of Respect

IBIZA

The most famous place to go clubbing on the planet can never quite lose its magic

Fittingly for an island named after the Ancient Egyptian god of dancing, no single spot on Earth collects more electronic music talent than summer in Ibiza. And the island's influence on global club culture has been huge – and recurring. From the early days of Balearic beat and the house boom of the '90s, to the way that DJs like Richie Hawtin and Sven Väth and the Circoloco Loco crew revitalised the flagging global scene in the mid '00s at marathon villa parties and sessions at DC10 with their adventures in minimal techno, Ibiza has long been both a microcosm of global club culture – and in its vanguard.

Clubs on the island have a heritage going back decades. The vast Privilege is the world's biggest with a capacity of 10,000, and possibly the only venue in the world where you can watch the sunrise inside a huge glass golf ball. Closed for 2022, its return will set the seal on the recovery from curfew and lockdown. Amnesia is a galleried colosseum of electronic music that holds 5,000 people and is the spiritual home of Väth's Cocoon parties. Pacha is the home of Marco Carola's Music On and Claptone's glamorous Masquerade. Others have built on what's gone before: Ushuaïa grew from a modest beach bar hosting parties by Luciano to a glitzy hotel with an attached daytime outdoor stage that has hosted everyone from Kraftwerk to Snoop Dogg to Pharell Williams, and features residencies from Calvin Harris and CamelPhat. Space Ibiza, formerly just across the road from Ushuaïa in Playa Den Bossa, was for generations of clubbers and visitors the paragon of the Ibiza club experience. Founded in 1989 in a former convention centre, it grew organically and spontaneously, sprawling over the site further each year, the music on its famous terrace pioneered by

Five-time winner of "Best Global Club" at the International Dance Music Awards, Ibiza's Space closed its doors in 2016

British DJs like Brandon Block and Alex P and replacing the (by then covered over) Amnesia outdoor area as the planet's must-visit al fresco club space. Its epic closing party in 2016 was one of the most epochal events of the decade in club culture as Space rounded up the DJs old and new who had contributed to its decades of incredible memories. Carl Cox – so intimately associated with the club for over 15 years – closing out the festivities with Angie Stone's "Wish I Didn't Miss You" as his last tune. The stunning Hï Ibiza, a custom-built, hi tech home for residencies from stars like Black Coffee and FISHER and the disco/house extravaganza of Glitterbox, rose from the hallowed ground in 2017.

But being the most famous place to go clubbing on the planet has its disadvantages, too. Ibiza is club culture commodified: besides being an incredible experience, its superclubs are ruthlessly efficient at turning passion – and hedonism – into euros. But people have probably been saying Ibiza's not as good as it used to be since the time of the pyramids. Somehow it still maintains its magic and its spirit. A night spent in the bars and restaurants stacked against the wall of the Old Town's citadel; a trip to the beaches in the magical north of the island; a beachfront lunch that somehow drifts beyond sunrise; a more informal club experience at peripheral venues like Underground or La Torre or Las Dalias; new nights like 2022's HE.SHE. THEY. at Amnesia with its laser focus on making clubland truly equal and accessible to everyone – there are a thousand ways to reconnect with what makes Ibiza unique.

Joseph Capriati behind the decks at DC10

Tania Vulcano
A key resident at DC10'a Circoloco since 1999, Uruguay-born Vulcano has been repping the deep, percussive end of techno ever since the club was little more than a Monday afterparty for the Island's diehards. Now she's in international demand, touring the world with Circoloco and playing across Ibiza throughout the year.

José Padilla
Padilla, playing at venues like Es Paradís and Café del Marin the late '80s and '90s, would become the world's foremost chill-out DJ. He also invented the chill-out compilation, though he began by selling illegal mixtapes, recounting, "I made 20 or 30 of them with a nice cover from a painter friend of mine. First day I went, I sell all of them. Next day I did double and sold them all again. Fuck! I buy another tape machine." Eventually, he flew to London with his mixtape and visited a few record companies. The first *Café del Mar* compilation sold 8,000 copies. By the fifth, sales were up to half a million.

Seamless Recordings
Helmed by Ibiza veteran Graham Sahara, Seamless showcases the chilled-out side of the island, releases from acts like Bryan Peroni, Sugarman and Javier Mio, exploring downtempo and organic house. Soundtrack to the sunset.

CLUB / EVENT

Underground Ibiza
Free to enter most nights, semi-outdoor and built around a traditional finca, Underground champions non-commercial sounds like the incredible tINI & Friends's nights of house and techno. It is a throwback to a different age.

Flash at Pikes
Just outside of tourist hotspot Sant Antoni, Pikes Hotel built its legend in the '80s as the location for wild parties for the likes of Freddie Mercury, and, of course, being the poolside setting for Wham's 'Club Tropicana' video. But it's also home to some cracking club nights and one-off parties, woven around its rickety network of bars and barns, with lots of space and scope for meeting the island's eccentrics and faces new and old. Flash is a determinedly inclusive night with a carnival atmosphere, including drag queens, dancers, an in-house opera singer and a music policy that puts the party first.

○ RECORD SHOP

MTM
With a sleek minimalist decor and a selection of new and second-hand vinyl, DJ essentials like cartridges, and even the odd bit of vintage production equipment, this Ibiza town store is the only one on the island. It was opened in 2018 by DJ and producer duo 2vilas, who once worked on the production team at Pacha. House predominates, and look out for releases on their own label and occasional in-store sessions.

ALFREDO

Ibiza's history as a place of refuge dates back millennia. First settled by Phoenician traders fleeing attacks by the brutal Assyrian Empire on their homeland of Lebanon around 2,800 years ago, it has been a sanctuary for Carthaginians, Romans, Spanish Jews fleeing the inquisition, modern artists fleeing the Nazis, and countless others. The story of Alfredo Fiorito, perhaps Ibiza's most famous DJ (and likely Europe's most influential) and Amnesia, the club where he made his name, is part of this pattern.

Alfredo was born in Rosario in Argentina in 1953, and by the age of 23 was working as a journalist, music critic and concert promoter. But in 1976, when a fascist military junta took over the country in a military coup, shutting down newspapers, persecuting psychologists, banning rock and roll and even long hair, he left his homeland and emigrated, first to the Spanish mainland and later to Ibiza.

He drifted around a succession of jobs including fashion designer, candle maker, delivery man and barman, and it was while working in a bar in Ibiza's Port in 1982 that he first tried his hand at DJing. In 1983, he was approached to play Amnesia. Originally a remote farmhouse refuge for American hippies who were fleeing the Vietnam War draft, Amnesia was once known as "The Workshop of Forgetfulness". By the mid-1980s it was an open air, white-walled venue set around a pool and surrounded by space-age geometric sculptures. Alfredo was soon playing seven hours a night, six nights a week. Having left Argentina an enthusiast for Jethro Tull and prog-rock, the anything-goes atmosphere at Amnesia, global influences, and the many hours to fill saw him expand his repertoire.

He played reggae, oddball pop and even *The Pink Panther Theme* alongside the new house music emerging from the US, creating a soundtrack that fitted the locale's balmy hedonism; an eclectic 'Balearic beat'. Meanwhile, Amnesia was becoming a playground for the international jet set fleeing the paparazzi or their own demons, from pop stars like Grace Jones and Duran Duran to artists, film directors and actors. And as Spain and the Balearic Islands became a newly affordable holiday option for the non-glitterati, they were joined on the dancefloor by not only the locals and Spanish mainlanders but by the Italians, French, Germans, Swiss, and the rest of Europe, not to mention Americans and Canadians. And of course, the Brits.

At the time, British nightclubs were more famed for drunken violence than the kind of stylish hedonism found at Amnesia. The mixture of nationalities, of straight, gay, Black, white, rich, poor, normal and hippies, found dancing together there was as much a revelation as the way Alfredo stitched together seamlessly so many types of music into a coherent vibe.

British DJs like Danny Rampling, Paul Oakenfold, Nancy Noise and many more visited Ibiza and Amnesia as tourists and left as missionaries. "Alfredo was the one who inspired the whole original wave of British and European DJs," says Rampling. "When I first saw and heard what he was doing in Ibiza I came straight back to the UK and started my own club, Shoom, and many others did the same. I'd been a funk and soul guy, and had been going nowhere, really, as a DJ for seven years. But when I heard what Alfredo was doing with house and Balearic music, I knew it was something I had to get involved in."

It wasn't just them, of course, and it wasn't just the British (a young Sven Väth was among those whose life changed direction after exposure to the '80s Ibiza scene). But when ecstasy hit Britain in the late '80s, the clubs founded by those directly inspired by Alfredo's dancefloor became the launchpad for the Second Summer Of Love, and an appreciative market for the new sounds coming from the US (often neglected in their homeland). They would in turn inspire more people from across Europe to build their own club culture in their own cities, and to revel in the refuge and freedom it offered.

BAR CEL ONA

A laid-back scene that's responsible for some of the world's most revered electronic music festivals

Barcelona's club and festival scene shows what happens when nightlife is celebrated as the life-affirming, economy-boosting, community-building phenomenon that we all know it is. A key catalyst of that is the Sónar festival every June, featuring a typically electronically inclined line-up that can range from The Chemical Brothers to Charlotte de Witte, alongside mind-blowing visual and multimedia artists. Sónar seems to have seeped into the DNA of a city that – with its weather, beaches, characterful neighbourhoods bursting with street art and a demographic of creative, beautiful, passionate people who love to stay up all night –was already inclined to greatness. "There's so much love that goes into the events and venues," says DJ Anja Schneider, who regularly hosts her Mobilee label parties across the city.

The number of electronic festivals that the city enjoys each year is breathtaking. Take November's MIRA festival, set in a converted 19th-century textile factory and showcasing the frontier of electronic music and digital arts. Or the more straightforward rave-up of DGTL Barcelona, with an annual line-up of techno's biggest hitters: Hawtin, Tale Of Us et al. There are the stunning events at El Monasterio, set in the picture-perfect courtyards of the Poble Espanyol architectural park, including in 2022 a Detroit Love showcase from Carl Craig. And of course, there's Primavera Sound each June, where live electronic acts and DJs have as much headline prominence as the international 'rawk' and indie bands.

But festivals and events in offbeat spaces aren't all that keeps Barcelona's scene ticking over. It's the clubs that maintain the vibe year-round. There's Nitsa, aka the Apolo, a favourite with local resident Maceo Plex. There's the tiny Moog, tucked behind the somewhat dodgy streets of the lower Las Ramblas and dripping with history. And of course, there's Razzmatazz, more than 20 years strong and still the vanguard of club culture and live music in the city.

If it's your first time in Barcelona there are a few things to remember. Don't leave valuables on an outdoor café table or not securely tucked in your pocket. Become familiar with the public transport system or take water and walking shoes to any Sónar event, because taxis somehow become rarer than unicorn spoor. Also, bear in mind that the idea of 'getting in the club early' is definitely not a thing here. Your favourite DJ will not be playing before midnight, and no one you want to meet will be on time. Try to relax into it ("'tranquillo!") and enjoy some of the best food on the planet and the bars in neighbourhoods like Gràcia and El Born.

DJS

Zora Jones
Born in Austria, DJ, producer and visual artist Jones made the eminently sensible move to Barcelona aged 20, where she and partner/collaborator Sinjin Hawke continue to push boundaries with their Fractal Fantasy label. Check out the pair's mind-blowing AV show at Sónar where they're perennial favourites.

Coyu
The Catalan DJ and producer runs the Suara label and clothing brand from its HQ in Barcelona. If Suara's output revolves around booming, big room techno, there is a fluffier edge to the project – a rescue centre for some of the city's unwanted cats. And yes, they are all named after DJs.

John Talabot
Barcelona-born Talabot's understated yet deeply melodic house and techno has a hugely loyal following in Spain and across Europe, particularly at Amsterdam's Dekmantel (he played the very first launch). His 2013 DJ-Kicks comp remains an absolute tour de force.

CLUBS / EVENT

Razzmatazz
A clubbing colossus that from the outside looks as if it's been dropped from space into the industrial area of Poblenou, Razzmatazz has an indoor festival vibe with five rooms of often wildly differing sounds, plus two outdoor terraces. Our tip is Lola's, the red-lit micro club that seems to have a gift for booking breakthrough DJs and artists just milliseconds before the hype goes nuclear.

Moog
Compact, dark and intense, the two-storey Moog has been the throbbing heartbeat of Barcelona's underground (albeit with an inclination to disco and '80s pop in the upstairs 'mirror room') all night, seven nights a week since 1996. Built on the site of a former cabaret bar in one of the city's edgiest districts, Wednesday is traditionally the night for international visitors – but the excellent residents never let standards slip.

Primavera Sound
The Barcelona edition of this globe-trotting festival takes place in the sprawling space age brutalism of the quayside Parc del Fòrum over 10 days in June. Sixteen arenas, from colossal main stages to quirky beach pop-ups, are connected by walkways and flyovers. Packed with huge international and local acts, it's worth exploring in full.

Amelie Lens performing at OFFSonar

O RECORD SHOP

Discos Paradiso
Opened in 2010, for proof of the impact of this emporium of new and second-hand electronica, just check out the wall of Polaroids behind the cash desk featuring both the shop's squadron of DJs and the international stars who've dropped in for a specially arranged showcase.

Mall Grab performing at Razzmatazz

LISBON

Europe's musical melting pot, Lisbon's diaspora fuels its uniqueness, drawing musicians and DJs from all over the world

Thriving music scenes and nightlife, low rents and good weather have prompted a surge in the number of musicians and DJs moving to Lisbon, both from former Portuguese colonies in Africa and South America and from places like London, Berlin, Paris and New York. The melting pot of influences at this global maritime hub, once at the centre of Portugal's far-flung colonial empire, has fired new influences and styles.

House and techno may still be the main soundtrack, but more than a decade since Lisbon's distinctive blend of African and Latin-influenced electronica first started making waves internationally, the city is still riding a surge of musical activity. Innovators like DJ Marfox and the live act Buraka Som Sistema, who both made groundbreaking releases in the mid-2000s, paved the way for a new army of bedroom producers and professional musicians to meld the music of the city's migrant communities with Western electronic sounds. Artists such as Nidia Minaj, Pedro and DJ Nigga Fox gained global recognition for experimental tracks that use elements of genres like kuduro, kizomba and funaná. Lisbon's boom in Afro-electronic music has eroded some of the social barriers between the city and the ghettos on its peripheries. For more than a decade, DJ Marfox, one of the original pioneers of the distinctive diaspora-influenced batida sound, struggled to get booked by the clubs in the centre of the city. "My music was associated with poverty and crime," he says. It was only in 2014 when Príncipe started its monthly club night at Musicbox that things changed. "Now, DJs from the ghetto are spending months away from home, flying all around the world to play in clubs and at festivals."

The city's own festival scene is strong, with the 2022 addition of Sonár joining events like ID NO LIMITS, which attracts the likes of Arca alongside local DJs, and Lisb-ON, which takes place in Parque Eduardo VII in the heart of the city and in 2020 welcomed Jeff Mills and Peggy Gou. Yearly festival Ano 0 showcases experimental and outsider artists, fashion and new genres of

A summery crowd at Lisb-ON festival

music, and takes place across a weekend at two venues, starting Friday at Galleria Zé dos Bois, before shifting the next night to a converted fire house, ADAO, across the river in the nearby satellite town of Barreiro.

A unique feature of the Lisbon club scene, pioneered initially by scene dynamos Violet and Photonz at community radio station Rádio Quântica, is venues and promotions applying for arts council funding as a 'cultural association', with any profits put back into the project. Galleria Zé dos Bois and Núcleo A70 are among the DIY style venues that benefit from this arrangement, for years the preserve of orchestras and theatre companies. It's crucial in a city with few private investors.

Lisbon has, to put it mildly, a late-night culture: dancefloors at venues like Lux Frágil or Village Underground won't start to fill up until 3am. Time beforehand is spent in bars in neighbourhoods like Graça and Arroios, restaurant and music venues like Damas or perhaps having a late meal at home.

An Enchufada label showcase at B.Leza by the riverside in Lisbon

O RECORD SHOP

Flur Discos
This historic store in Arroios stocks everything from classics to off-kilter experimental. The first Lisbon outlet for UK labels like Hyperdub, they also stock reissue labels like Dark Entries and experimental sounds from the US. The atmosphere may be a little serious, but the curation is impeccable, and its focus is unmoved by trends and fashion.

Carl Craig behind the decks at Lisb-ON festival

Violet

Whether through her partnership with Photonz at Radio Quantica, her Naive record label and nights at Lux, or her workshops with local promoters and artists, Violet is a huge driving force behind Lisbon's rise to club culture powerhouse. But she's also one of Portugal's greatest DJ/producer exports, blending techno with everything from UK bass to avant-garde acid, and in demand from Berlin to Brazil.

Principé Discos

The sound of Lisbon's diasporic melting pot, committed to releasing music from the city's "suburbs, projects & slums", Principé introduced the world to the sound of Lisbon's barrios with its first release by co-founder Marfox. It has since showcased a constantly evolving fusion of gritty dancefloor-focused beats, avant-garde electronica and African and South American influences by artists like Nídia and DJ Nigga Fox.

Lux Fragil

The most famous and established club in Lisbon. With three large floors (the middle floor is house, downstairs is techno, the rooftop is laid back), Lux is lush, expensive by local standards, and attracts a clientele that spans generations, as well as tourists. Nevertheless, it still brings the electronic music community together regularly thanks to an expansive international booking policy, an incredible sound system, nights like Naive, which bring through new and interesting artists, and a dancefloor that can become a microcosm of the scene (even including a queer corner" says Violet, "on the front right-hand side").

Mina

This self-defined "techno underground clubbing scene for sexual and gender liberation" toured various Lisbon venues – including a strip bar and a gym– before finding a home on the second floor of a huge factory building near Lisbon Airport. It is one of the few events that locals will get to early, thanks to its runaway (runway?) popularity.

MILAN

From Fashion Week to Futurist industrial spaces, squat parties
to reggaeton, clubbing in Milan never goes out of style

While historically Rimini, seaside birthplace of Italo Disco, has been the
epicentre of electronic music in Italy, these days Milan – the fashion capital of
Europe, situated in the industrial heartland of the country – leads the way. Expo
2015, a World's Fair type showcase of global design and architecture held north
of the city, was the catalyst for Milan to explore the potential of its many
industrial spaces to host events and concerts. Its world-famous fashion and
design weeks are when the biggest DJ names descend on the city's clubs.

Amnesia Milano, out towards Linate airport, is the vanguard of the club scene,
also hosting monthly events in the massive Fabrique, a gigantic box of a 3,000
capacity-venue in an industrial zone a short walk south of the club, with names
like Boris Brejcha. Fabrique also used to host concerts and reggaeton nights
like the lively Mamacita. And as spring turns to summer, Social Music City kicks
into action with DJs from local legends Tale Of Us to Richie Hawtin and
promoters from Elrow to Circoloco split across two stages (indoor and outdoor
– Milan is not renowned for great weather). Tunnel, a railway arch venue is
another impressive space; look out for long-running Saturday residents night
Take it Easy, techno, house and disco with Bugsy and co., and guests like
Perlon's Zip.

On the far side of the airport you'll find Circolo Magnolia in Idroscalo Park, a
two-roomclub that expands to include outdoor stages in summer and attracts
some top international names like Dave Clarke and Boys Noize. Volt, back
towards the centre and the historic Basilica, is an intense rave box with LED
strips on the ceiling that seem to accelerate the dancefloor towards DJs like
Mind Against and Adriatique.

This is, of course, a fashion city, and it was only a decade ago that clubs would
not accept people with trainers on. While dress codes are pretty relaxed these
days, some effort and a little style is important – though nothing will guarantee
entry for male clubbers as much as turning up with female company in tow.

The outdoor stage at Tempio del Futuro Perduto

Make friends at daytime hangout/brunch spot Sanctuary Milan or at aperitivo time in neighbourhoods like Navigli or the Corso Como/Porta Garibaldi.

Plastic, once hailed as Milan's Studio 54 thanks to its stylish crowd and severe door pickers, has a new owner and a new venue but is still an interesting place to connect with a more old-school Milanese vibe, while Navigli's Apollo, attached to a stylish cocktail bar and bistro, has hosted Boiler Room events and has an adventurous booking policy that ranges from Ivan Smagghe to Djrum. If you really want to show off your glad rags, Just Cavalli, owned by the fashion designer, occasionally mixes up its commercial bookings with more interesting names, especially during Fashion Week, where you might catch South Africa's Themba aka Euphonik or a proper house set from Bob Sinclar. Milan's metro closes at 12.30am and most clubbers get to the venue at 1am by taxi (which is an expensive way to travel... Uber even more so) or by car, with the guests usually starting at 2am. By 4am, most start to drift off, usually to enjoy a surprisingly gourmet panini sandwich from the city's justly famed all-night food trucks before heading home.

Milan's home-grown talent, Tale of Us

◯ RECORD SHOP

Serendeepity

Serendeepity brings together music, design and art in a bright and quirky store that features furniture, books and instruments – and, this being Milan, there's also a vintage clothing section – alongside rare vinyl and the latest in techno, house and breakbeat. The shop celebrated 10 years of business in 2021 by releasing an EP featuring new music from San Proper and Fabrizio Mammarella.

Loco Dice behind the decks at Fabrique Milano

Tale Of Us

They may be Berlin-based now, but since their breakthrough in 2015 with tracks like dancefloor-hammering techno groove of 'Astral' (with Mind Against), remixes for Caribou, Plastikman, Kiasmos and Barnt, and DJ sets that find the perfect balance between immersive warehouse techno party and evocative IDM experience, duo Carmine Conte and Matteo Milleri are Milan's proudest DJ export and a guaranteed sell out on their return to the city.

Brina Knauss

Born in Slovenia, Knauss moved to Milan in the 2010s to pursue a modelling career before throwing it over in 2012 in favour of DJing. Playing across the city at clubs like Amnesia, by 2018 she had caught the ear of the likes of Luciano and Damian Lazarus, and has since played across the world, from Berlin's Watergate to the beach parties of Tulum, Mexico. She's also released on Rebellion and Frau Blau, her productions often featuring her own vocals.

Apparel

Founded by Giuseppe D'Alessandro (aka Kisk) in 2009 to push the boundaries of electronic music with new and diverse styles, Apparel releases artists and tracks from across the musical spectrum (from Fred P to Barcelona's Babsy), linked by a connection to house music that's sometimes tenuous, and a jazz sensibility that's absolutely essential. "Only jazz beats can bring a more human dynamic to cold electronic music," says Kisk. The label has its own avatar in the form of 'artist' Apparel Wax, brought to life by a collective of unnamed ghost producers, and even a line of personalised sake.

Amnesia Milano

A stylish, sleek industrial space of steel and anthracite (with waterfalls behind the two bars), Amnesia has space for 2,000 across its two rooms, with a custom RCF sound system in each. The club hosts big international guests like The Blessed Madonna and Kolsch almost every week, alongside local talents like Olympe and Brina Knauss.

Kappa FuturFestival

It might be in Turin (an hour from Milan on the fastest train), but worth mentioning how in the Parco Dora, a former industrial area that has been transformed into a stunning Futurist inspired mega sculpture, Kappa Futur takes place amid the storeys-high skeleton of a sheet metal plant, massive rusting hulks of warehouse supports and cooling towers. Carl Cox, Richie Hawtin, Dubfire, Charlotte de Witte, Jamie Jones, Seth Troxler, HAAi and Red Axes have all played across its four stages, with 25,000 attending the festival on each of its three days in July.

Parco Dora, a former industrial area near Turin that has been transormed into a Futurist-inspired megasculpture, and the site of Kappa FuturFestival

131

TEMPIO DEL FUTURO PERDUTO

Alongside Milan's legal club scene runs a parallel universe of squat parties and occupied spaces that offer a nightlife alternative for the city's student and countercultural population. While these are sometimes criticised by the city's promoters for swerving tax and safety regulations (as well as Italy's onerous performing rights fees), they're also where some of the most exciting and future-facing innovations in the city's club culture happen. None more so than Tempio del Futur Perduto (Temple of Lost Futures).

Opened in January 2018, the labyrinthine complex occupies a former transport maintenance depot opposite the privileged plots of Monumental Cemetery, to the north of downtown Milan. A ramshackle building, it is many things to many people, but the goal is singular: to repair cracks in Italian society by establishing a community built on acceptance, creativity, passion, and beats.

To attend one of the LGBTQ+ positive parties held each Friday and Saturday night, punters are encouraged to contribute something to wear or read, alongside a €5 entrance fee. Items in the former category are given to the most vulnerable; literature is free to take from the on-site library area near the entrance. "We talked a lot of times with politicians and institutions, but in the end they still preferred to leave it abandoned. So we got inside and began to work on the building without permission," explains Tempio's Tommaso Dapri, who cut his teeth in club promotion before moving into increasingly clandestine projects.

Tempio has since become a mecca for alternative culture, its interior transformed with new walls, toilets and wiring. Visuals by RE_light collective, aka Stefano Barbieri and Diego Longoni, involve crimson lasers striking the back wall. Strip beams are embedded within old tram lines that still score the floor. Framing the booth, a giant pyramid supports spots and strobes. Part club, part music production facility, it's also home to a dance studio, African drumming school, self-defence training gym, and a vinyl store. Footfall outside the space has increased significantly as a result, changing the image of a street once known only for prostitution and drugs.

"There are no guarantees here," Dapri says, explaining that everything has been funded by the parties. Their efforts have won over local residents, confused police

Crate-diggers browse the vinyl market at Tempio Del Futuro Perudto

and led the council to leave them alone – for now, at least. "We are working like a legal venue – CCTV and security. The craziest thing is that for every party, we even have an ambulance on standby. When the cops first came, they said to each other, 'It's a squat: stay safe, be alert'. They came in and were like, 'What the fuck is this place?'"

It's a place that attracts DJs like France's GiGi FM, Leo Mas, Or:la and even live shows from acts like Curses, as well as pioneering hybrid IR/metaverse events and installations where partygoers are invited to navigate characters through abstract landscapes, explore immersive worlds through VR headsets, or step into motion sensitive environments. Tempio was also the location for the world's longest DJ live stream event, spanning 340 hours and featuring DJ sets from Neil Landstrumm, Fabrizio Rat, Enrico Sangiuliano and more, alongside dial-ins from a host of promoters, artists and cultural figures from across Italy and the world, testifying to the post-Covid reality.

BRUSSELS

A recent renaissance in the Belgian capital has turned it into a club culture Centraal Station

After years of existing in the shadow of Amsterdam, Brussels' underground scene truly exploded in 2018 with two pivotal moments. The first was the opening of Kiosk Radio station, which became not just a showcase for local DJs and artists, but also a hangout spot and a hub for swapping ideas and coming together. At the height of lockdown, it assumed an almost symbolic role, as carefully distanced clubbers gathered outside during the day to hear the station's output through speakers on the street.It joined the recently opened Crevette Records shop just down the street, Brussels' first store for house, techno and experimental sounds in years, and another focal point for the burgeoning community.

And then there was the opening of C12 (usually pronounced in its French form to sound a bit like 'seduce'): a new 900-capacity, two-room club that would share the burden with the long-running Fuse, while also giving its established rival an infusion of new energy and a wider talent pool. C12 is ambitiously built in and around a working entrance to the Centraal Train Station (the club races to set up their own entrance when the station thoroughfare closes at 7pm), a stunning space designed by modernist/ art nouveau architect Victor Horta in 1910. The club even incorporates a vintage wooden escalator. Crucially, in this dense city, it also means no neighbours to make noise complaints.

Combined with a new embrace of nightlife by the city authorities, the effect was almost immediate. Brussels' community of club collectives, from the long-established Deep in House, who took over the creation of C12, to newer crews like Not Your Techno and Under My Garage, had an ecosystem to work within. The yearly Listen! Festival, held across multiple venues, from Fuse to collaborations with warehouse party crew Hangar, is the perfect showcase for them, bringing together collectives and DJs from across the city and the wider country. The pandemic saw Fuse and C12 each put their energies into developing their own strong pool of local residents to supplement their regular international guests – think Ben UFO or Rødhåd for Fuse, Saoirse or Tama Sumo for C12. A 20-minute walk from each other in the city centre, both clubs have a broad underground music policy, and are open on Friday and Saturday nights until between 6am and 8am.

Beforehand, locals hang out and drink the cheap but amazing beer in neighbourhoods like Saint-Gillesand Ixelles or downtown, home to DJ bars like Bonnefooi, renowned for marathon DJ sets that can last from midnight till mid-morning. Getting around Brussels is pretty straightforward, though it's night buses only after midnight and the polyglot local pronunciations can make asking directions a bit of a lottery, which concert venue Beursschouwburg cheekily acknowledges with its sign featuring about 20 different ways to spell its name.

A solo dancer at C12

DJS / LABEL

LeFtO
A long-time collaborator with Gilles Peterson, LeFtO is a living legend in Belgium, where for 20 years he hosted a show on the country's top popular music radio station. A tirelessly eclectic DJ whose selections range across genres, time periods and countries, LeFtO is an evangelist for his home city, to the extent that he made national news when he jumped ship to join Kiosk radio.

Walrus
A key figure in the Brussels scene for many years, Walrus not only plays across the city but is starting to build international recognition, regularly appearing on line-ups in Berlin. He runs deep digging record label Basic Moves, but also has a side gig building beautifully unique record and deck shelves and stands for Brussel's DJs. Think Charles Eames meets Nicolas Lutz.

Sara Dziri
Founder of club crew Not Your Techno, Belgian-Tunisian Dziri is a resident at Fuse, and a regular at Kiosk and C12. Her atmospheric yet firmly dancefloor-focused recent album for Glasgow's Optimo label, *Close To Home*, should see her going global very soon.

Crammed Discs
A pillar of Brussels' music scene since its founding in 1981, Crammed's focus on adventurous music from Belgium and worldwide, whether indie, electronic, rock or pop, has had a global impact. Its releases by Israeli rock band Minimal Compact, for example, were a huge influence on James Murphy's LCD Soundsystem and his own DFA label, while sub label SSR Records, active between 1988 and the mid 2000s, charted a course between house, new beat, acid, future jazz, broken beat, drum'n'bass, hip-hop, rave and trance with groundbreaking releases from the likes of Herbert and Carl Craig.

CLUBS

Fuse
Since 1994, Fuse, a former 1920s cinema, has spearheaded the local scene. A small wall of fame in one of the back rooms boasts a litany of artists who performed there in the 1990s, including Carl Craig, Richie Hawtin, Aphex Twin, Daft Punk and even Björk, in 1997. "We have always had a very solid formula and we never deviate from our programming," says former managing director Olivier Ramoudt. "When trance and drum'n'bass were hot, we didn't join in that trip." It isn't all techno, of course – look out for the likes of Peggy Gou and Mall Grab dropping by.

La Cabane
This 200-cap venue on the outskirts of the city near the breathtaking Sonian Forest is another new arrival, a wood panelled, low-ceilinged box venue that can shift from loungey cocktail bar to rave bunker in the space of a few moments. Look out for great local DJs like Kong and guest visits from the likes of Antal.

O RECORD SHOP

Crevette
Besides its great selection of underground electronic music, including an Aladdin's cave of used vinyl overseen lovingly by DJ Walrus, Crevette organises parties and events, has a distribution arm, and was a catalyst for the opening of Kiosk and C12 two years after its own launch in 2016.

AMS TER DAM

Moonlight bike rides and the massive ADE are among the highlights of one of the best cities for clubbing on the planet

It may lack the underground patina of Berlin or the long heritage of London, but Amsterdam is always in the conversation when it comes to discussing the best cities for clubbing in the world. And it's a conversation the city embraces, perhaps keen to transition away from fame – and tourism – based on coffee shops and red-light districts.

No event has done more to raise the profile of Amsterdam within the global club culture than the astonishing Amsterdam Dance Music Event (ADE). Starting off as an industry conference in 1996, it's become one of the world's biggest parties: five days of club events, panel discussions and networking, including showcases from labels, parties and artists from across the world. There's even an Amsterdam outpost of Barcelona's DGTL festival at the NDSM Docklands site, a chilly yet invigorating ferry ride from Centraal Station.

The rise of ADE, the city leaning in to club culture, and a local crowd that's wildly enthusiastic and educated about electronic music (with a strong heritage in trance, techno and hardcore) has spurred the creation of incredible venues across the city. Some of these are truly epic, like Gashouder, a huge circular chamber that forms the centrepiece of Awakenings Festival, with the biggest names in house and techno from Adam Beyer to Tale of Us. De Marktkantine is another, a sprawling converted theatre that hosts shows, as well as gigantic concert venue Paradiso, built into a converted church.

Others are simply unique. The RADION is an industrial-style 24-hour venue residing in the old dentistry academy building, showcasing queer facing rave crews like De Reünie. Shelter is a high-tech bunker venue underneath the landmark A'DAM Tower. There's the ephemeral Sociëteit SEXYLAND, a highly conceptual temporary club based on a boat with a different promoter every night, 365 nights a year. Faralda Crane Hotel is a micro-club and living space suspended 50 metres above the docklands in a converted crane, where *Mixmag* has thrown ADE parties and live streams.

Then there are well-loved spaces, like perky late night bar/club Disco Dolly, multi-room concert venue Melkweg and Warehouse Elementenstraat, which hosted some of the first illegal raves in Holland, all pillars of the scene for years in their own way. Amsterdam is also the home of Dekmantel Festival, held in August in the green fields of the Amsterdamse Bos, a five-day showcase of the best of Europe's underground scene, from Batu to Doppplereffekt to Laurel Halo.

Amsterdam is compact, fantastic fun to walk around thanks to its architecture and canals, and has a very good transport system. But you already know the best way to get about. Nothing beats a moonlit bike ride to the club – just make sure that if you're a pedestrian near a bike lane, you look both ways for two-wheeled danger. In a collision with one of those basketed steel behemoths, there is only ever one winner.

DJS / LABEL

Carista
Born in Utrecht to parents from Suriname, Carista won a DJ competition in Rotterdam before taking up the craft as a career. Soon she found herself playing Dutch festivals from Lowlands to Down The Rabbit Hole and Appelsap, taking up a residency on London's influential NTS radio and playing clubs like Secretsundaze. "Musically, the mix of Detroit house, UK broken-beat vibes and bass stuff she plays is totally fitting with Secretsundaze," says the club's Giles Smith. "I could see someone with authenticity who is completely natural behind the decks."

Job Jobse
Making his name at the much missed Trouw (he first took to the decks there before beginning a residency that often included marathon six-hour sets), Jobse's musical style, gleefully weaving between house, disco, techno, acid, deep house and everything in between, have led to stops at Panorama Bar, fabric and at the biggest festivals all over the world, especially alongside regular b2b sparring partner Dixon.

Armada Music
Starting out as a trance-led outlet, Armada has spread its wings over the past 10 years to cover a wide range of styles, building an empire of sub labels and working with house legends and rising underground talents such as ANOTR. Thanks to Armin van Buuren, one of the best loved artists in dance music, its worldwide events schedule offers up many of the hottest tickets in dance music, from the large-scale Armada Beach bash in Argentina to the intimate Armada Invites showcases in the label's own club, constructed in its hometown Amsterdam location.

CLUBS

Shelter
Located underground and accessed via a hatch in the floor below the A'DAM Tower, Shelter is a sanctuary for the best underground music in the city. Focusing on extended sets rather than packing the bill with multiple names, the club regularly welcomes the biggest and best in dance music, such as Robert Hood, Zip, Peggy Gou and Mall Grab. There's one room of music, so no maze-like complex to navigate: just a big space with an even bigger Funktion-One sound system.

BRET
Amsterdam's hottest day party venue is an indoor space transformed into a red-lit mystical jungle with plants and foliage. Open Saturday and Sunday, sound tracked by local crews like the housey SlapFunk, Italo fanatics Disco Total and guests like AMORAL and Joseph Capriati, it also has a strong social purpose. Part of the proceeds from every DAYCARE party goes to a charity picked by one of the headliners/curators.

Slapfunk at Shelter, Amsterdam's (literally) underground sanctuary for electronic music

○ RECORD SHOP

Rush Hour Records
Co-founded by DJ Antal, and an incubator for local and global DJ talent including Hunee, Tom Trago and San Proper, Rush Hour Records is the 'Dam's most famous record shop. It truly comes alive at ADE time, when it hosts in-store sessions from the biggest DJs in the world. Look out also for their takeovers of venues like Manchester's Warehouse Project.

THE NIGHT MAYOR OF AMSTERDAM

Why did it take so long to think of it? The idea of appointing an experienced, accountable figure to interface between resident groups, local businesses, authorities, and the stakeholders in the nightlife economy seems obvious now, but it wasn't until 2016, when Amsterdam appointed its first Night Mayor, that the idea was put in practice.

Mirik Milan, a 35-year-old former club promoter, was appointed the first *nachtburgemeester* of Amsterdam after being selected by public vote, and soon got to work reconciling the daytime and nocturnal sides of the city's economy. His first job was to change the way decisions were made. The city's response to any problem with nightlife, he told the *Guardian*, was to "bring in a curfew, tighten regulations, shut places down, ban stuff. It's understandable: how can you make good laws if you're in city hall, with no real clue of what's happening out there in the night-time? The only way is for the night economy, city hall and residents to figure out, together, how to make it work".

Milan introduced a scheme to spread nightlife outside the city centre, offering 24-hour licences to venues like De School in the suburbs. By expanding the use of these licences inside the city too, he tackled the mass exodus to Amsterdam's narrow streets that was caused by all clubs closing at the same time. Stewards in the centre helped the inebriated and the lost, while keeping a typically Dutch (friendly yet phlegmatic) eye out for trouble. Even the lighting around the streets was changed, from a confrontational glare to a more relaxed glow.

And it has worked. Amsterdam's streets are safer, its businesses and residents happier, and its club scene healthier. Milan has since moved on from the position, replaced by former journalist Ramon de Lima. Now Milan advocates for nightlife globally and advises the many other cities around the world who've enthusiastically embraced the concept. The risk is that without the power and trust that Amsterdam invested in its Night Mayor, they end up little more than a flak catcher, or a lightning rod for the frustrations of venue owners and clubbers. Hopefully cities like London and Washington DC, who've appointed their own equivalents, can prove that, unlike wooden shoes or sweet mayonnaise on French fries, the idea can make sense outside of Holland.

Amsterdam's Night Mayor even changed the street lighting to make it more relaxed

ROT TER DAM

Across a selection of unique venues and event spaces, Holland's other city likes its music hard and fast

Rotterdam is a city of doers, makers, free-thinkers and pioneers. As a port city, it's not only industrial (and industrious); it's also one of the most multicultural and architecturally interesting hubs in Europe. After the city centre was bombed flat during WWII, Rotterdam became an architectural playground resulting in quirky buildings like the giant Lego brick-like Markthal, the disorientating Cube Houses and the towering Pencil (*Potlood* in Dutch), all fighting for space in a city that has been in a state of perpetual redevelopment for the last 70 years.

Once an international clubbing destination with superclubs like Las Palmas in the '80s, the explosion of gabber culture in the 1990s transformed stately villa-turned-discotheque Parkzicht into one of the most notorious venues on the planet. Alongside gabber, Rotterdam has been a crucible for techno since the very beginning, with DJs like Michel de Hey and Speedy J flying the flag. Holland's second-largest city certainly has a rich history of dance music, and yet its club culture has been in steep decline since the mid-2000s due to dwindling venue capacity. But there is plenty going on, if you know where to look.

The best known clubs are city centre-based, like techno hotspots Cultuurpodium Perron and nearby Toffler, housed in an old pedestrian tunnel beneath the bustling streets near Central Station. One of the most impressive is the 5,000-capacity event venue the Maassilo, a former grain silo across the iconic Erasmus Bridge in Rotterdam South. On the 10th floor of the Maassilo, and accessible only by elevator, is the revived Now&Wow Club, a Rotterdam institution from the 2000s, which today hosts a variety of club nights including the drum'n'bass party Korsakov and local DJ Cynthia Spiering's techno party Courtoisy. There's the alternative event space WORM, located on the hip, bar-lined Witte de Withstraat and made exclusively from salvaged materials, which has one of the city's most diverse range of musical programming, from hip-hop to vogue dance nights. Its affiliated bar, Wunderbar, serves strictly vegan junk food and locally sourced beers, and tucked away along a side street there's the tiny Performance Bar, fronted by the maverick performing artist and DJ Daan Draait, which programs a weekly range of performative, inclusive and queer-friendly nights.

For a real taste of Rotterdam, catch a tram, metro, or bus – or better yet, hire a bike from Central Station – and visit the Rotterdam Makers District in Rotterdam West. Here, artist studios and workshops are quenched by Bohemian bars and restaurants offering club alternatives, including the not-quite-legal Keilecafe, and Weelde, which has an indoor skatepark and an outdoor beach bar hosting a vibrant program of local DJs and crews, like the breakbeat-touting No Friends Collective and Malafide Records. In Rotterdam West you can also find the city's first new club venue in far too long, the 24-hour-licensed Club BIT, which has become a place for more immersive forms of house and techno, delivered by locals like Ofra, Fenna Fiction and Alberta Balsam, as well as visiting tastemakers from neighbouring cities The Hague and Amsterdam.

○ RECORD SHOP

Clone.nl

Rotterdam's quintessential record store for the heads, run by local legend Serge, Clone Records has been the supplier of the very best in underground dance music since 1992. A cornerstone of the dance community, Clone is located under the arches of a disused railway line in an area called the Hofbogen in Rotterdam North, close to jazz, soul and funk venue BIRD (who also serve some of the best pizzas in town).

The iconic Maassilo, a venue and events space on the site of a former grain silo

DJS / LABEL

Benny Rodrigues aka ROD

One of Holland's hardest-working DJs, often playing several gigs across the country every single weekend, is the born and bred Rotterdammer Benny Rodrigues. A music obsessive who DJs every conceivable genre under his own name (and strictly techno as ROD), Rodrigues started out as a teenager replacing Tiësto at the counter of the record store Basic Beat. He rose to prominence as a resident of Now&Wow in the '90s, and he's not stopped since.

Jetti

Jetti Steffers has been a driver of Rotterdam nightlife for many years from behind the scenes as one of the co-founders of BAR (now known as POING). Teaming up with long-time friend and colleague Sjoerd Post as the DJ duo Jetti & Post, recently she's been striking out on her own, playing across the Low Countries and in Berlin clubs like Renate.

PRSPCT Recordings

Founded in 2002 from a drum'n'bass party series at the historic venue Nighttown by the DJ and hardcore punk guitarist and singer Thrasher, PRSPCT Recordings is the home of rebellious, hard electronic music of all styles. PRSPCT has become a Rotterdam institution in its own right, hosting one of the city's biggest annual club events at the Maassilo and exporting their sound to the world via regular label nights with its eclectic resident DJs Rudi Ratte and Li-Z.

CLUB / EVENT

Perron

For banging underground techno (and more) there's only one spot in the harbour city with a regular weekend club program: Perron. Residents include Abstract Division and their DECODE series, as well as Marsman's scuzzier Pinkman label nights. Local talents Stranger, Thanos Hana and Lenson are also Perron favourites. Situated a mere five minutes walk from Central Station, next to live concert venue Annabel, the seasonal Biergarten, the tiny record store Pinkman, Operator Radio's container HQ, and the arcade hall-cum-basement club POING, everything you need for a great day and night out in Rotterdam is right here in the Schieblock complex.

Blijdorp Festival

For electronic music, Blijdorp Festival is one of the city's best for showcasing home-grown talent and a sense of community-building across Rotterdam's various musical factions. A one-day event happening in August at Roel Langerakpark, it leans on the sunnier side of house, funk, disco and electro via locals like Philou Louzolo, David Vunk and Benny Rodrigues.

BERLIN

More than just 'techno Valhalla', Berlin's politicised
and superabundant club culture is unique to the city

A banner by Rirkrit Tiravanija reading "Morgen ist die frage" ("Tomorrow is the question") hangs across Berghain's entrance

We need to talk about door policy. The careful curation of their crowd by the door staff at most of Berlin's myriad underground clubs has perhaps shaped the rhythm and culture of the city's nightlife more than anything since techno first reached the city in the '80s. Outside the club, the risk of not getting in means that many locals go out alone, avoiding the very real possibility (not considered a moral dilemma here at all) of having to ditch their friends and proceed solo. Locals also tend to avoid Saturday nights, when queues can be four hours long, in favour of starting their weekend after Sunday brunch. Though those same lengthy queues can take on their own vibe and social community – and the occasional person reading a book in the line. Door policies can be open to abuse, with persistent allegations down the years of racial profiling and even quotas, especially on non-white foreigners. Indeed, in the spirit of Chic writing 'Le Freak' as a response to a knock-back from New York's Studio 54 (the original lyrics were "Fuck Off!"), there are club promoters in Berlin – like activist fetish crew Gegen – who've been inspired to start their own events simply because they struggled to get into existing parties.

Unlike in many other cities, bar hopping before a night out doesn't really make sense for a number of reasons: the marathon all-weekend opening hours, the need to be compos mentis for the door staff and mindful of your stamina, and, of course, because time spent bar hopping means waiting longer to get in the club. And while neighbourhoods like Neukölln, Alt-Treptow, Friedrichshain and Kreuzberg are bursting with great bars, restaurants and nightlife, why would you waste time bar hopping when clubs offer so much? Most have multiple rooms to explore, outdoor areas buzzing with people to meet, and food even (such as Berghain's famed ice cream parlour). And if you want to nip out for a *Döner* (Berlin has the best kebabs this side of the Bosphorus), your stamp will get you back in without needing to queue again.

Thanks to Berlin's door policies, clubs like OHM, KitKat, Renate, Ficken3000, Roses, Anomalie Art Club, Trauma Bar, Funkhaus, ://aboutblank and, of course, Berghain/Panorama Bar, the atmosphere inside is social, free, sexually liberated, and often politically active,and 'safe' in the best sense of the word. Female overseas visitors will often remark at the absence of the male gaze, never mind unwanted pestering.

And we haven't even mentioned the music! Still a magnet for producers and artists from all over the world–- it's been an incubator for the likes of Fidelity Kastrow, Somewhen and Delfonic –- Berlin's incredible pool of club residents somehow remains largely untapped globally, despite another artist seemingly breaking through every couple of months. It may be perceived as techno Valhalla, but the sound in the city is far more eclectic these days. More crews and nights have embraced an increasingly fluid approach to selection – look out for DJs like THC playing high-energy '90s house and trance at parties like Multisex or Byron Yeates's Radiant Love – but the underground remains the mainstream here: if you're looking for big room tech house and EDM, look elsewhere. The music, though, is a given. You go out in Berlin for a collective experience that reflects the needs of the community. And what you get is well worth queueing outside for a few hours.

Ellen Allien

The DJ, producer, musician and vocalist behind nearly a dozen albums and head of the BPitch label was playing legendary Berlin clubs like Tresor, Ostgut and Maria am Ostbahnhof as far back as 1992. At the forefront of global techno ever since, she's also a visible and powerful evangelist and guardian of the club culture of her native city – her 2017 *Nost* album was a nostalgic tribute to what she calls "the best city in the world."

Ben Klock

The Klockworks supremo did as much as anyone to take the new techno sound of Berlin (and Berghain, where he's been resident since 2005) international. Characterising his sets as banging techno, though, does the hard touring Berliner a disservice. Amid the thump is an open-minded ability to bring in other genres and a great deal of subtlety. And his breathtaking Photon AV show, which has visited Printworks in London and Amsterdam's Awakenings Festival, "combines light, music and architecture into a whole new multisensory experience," as he puts it.

PAN

A "multi-disciplinary record label and platform for artists" in the best Berlin tradition, Bill Kouligas's imprint has released everything from Objekt's deeply cinematic *Cocoon Crush* album (2018) to the sonic experimentalism of Yves Tumour, '70s avant-garde Bigaku school collective Marginal Consort, and even conceptual artists James Hoff and Mark Leckey. The label devotes as much attention to detail to the design of their beautiful physical releases as they do to pushing sonic boundaries.

CLUB

Panorama Bar

The archetype. Playing Berghain's upstairs room is the top of the bucket list for pretty much every DJ on the planet. Built inside a monolithic former energy plant on the border of Friedrichshain and Kreuzberg, you probably know the score: no photos, no mirrors, epic sunrises through the giant windows (when the shutters sporadically flash open), brutally selective door staff, and a galaxy class sound system. Many consider it the apex of the club experience.

Ellen Allien, a powerful evangelist and guardian of Berlin's club culture

○ RECORD SHOP

Elevate Berlin
Berlin institution since 1989, Hard Wax might be the most obvious choice, but Freidrichshain-based Elevate Berlin, owned and run by Berlin house and techno icon Cinthie, is a little gem, with a carefully compiled selection of underground house, techno, ambient and leftfield electronica and extremely desirable merch from in-house labels like Bestemodus.

Ben Klock, a resident of Berghain since 2005

THE LOVE PARADE

"Doobidoo doot doot baap bap". Da Hool's classic '90s trance banger, 'Meet Her At The Love Parade' is just one legacy of the Berlin event that captured the imagination of the world. Writer and historian Matthew Collin (*Altered States*, 1997), who was there for one of the early parades in 1992 describes it as:

"a gathering of the clans from across the recently reunited country to revel in the sheer exuberance of their own existence, to show off their extravagant beauty in all its polymorphous perversity... to stake a claim on the urban landscape not just as a place for buying and selling, but as the forum for a carnival: our carnival, with its youthful innocence that could not, and did not, last."

The Berlin Love parade started as one of those late-night projects that are usually forgotten in the harsh light of day. It was the brainchild of Matthias Roeingh, better known as Dr. Motte, a Berlin-born DJ who played in a punk band in the early '80s and then went on to run some of the city's first acid house clubs. He was inspired by a visit to England at the height of the acid house boom in 1988, where ravers in the UK's cities would flood out of shut down events to take over the street with their ghetto blasters, creating spontaneous outpourings of euphoria and dancing that baffled authorities, leaving them powerless in the face of so much concentrated youthful energy. Dr. Motte wondered if he could recreate the scene in Berlin. The idea was to bring Berlin's nocturnal subculture of freaks, weirdos and beautiful, smiling club people into the light on one of Berlin's busiest shopping streets for what Collins calls a "ravers' promenade."

The first one happened in 1989, with the city, its Western part long a refuge for European counterculture, still divided in two. It drew around 150 attendees. Motte chose "Friede, Freude, Eierkuchen" (Peace, Joy, Pancakes) as its motto. By registering The Love Parade as a political event and claiming it was a protest for peace and equitable food distribution, he cheekily dodged having to pay for policing or cleaning up. When the Wall fell in Berlin later that year, many young people felt the same way as West Berlin teenager Ellen Allien: "I finally felt free to start the life I wanted to, to build up all my ideas. Because the city was so full of pain from the war, I felt I needed to do something that made us happy, to help create a lifestyle that could find a place in society." Paging Dr. Motte.

Within a few years, attendance at the Love Parade had risen to 150,000, collected around a ragtag procession of DIY floats, dancers, techno vikings and semi-organised sound systems. By the end of the century, there were 1.5 million people from all over the world taking part in a commercialised event that had lost its anarchist, politicised spirit (some locals even set up their own annual counter-demonstration, the Fuckparade). Copycat events sprang up around the world for a short period – the 2000 UK Love Parade in Leeds, organised by BBC Radio 1, attracted an estimated 400,000 ravers.

The Berlin event petered out after 2010, when it was sold to a corporation and moved to a ticketed space in Duisburg with heartbreaking results: 41 died in a horrific and avoidable crush. But it had set a template for the city that still resonates to this day. Berlin's civic pride in its 'night people', its subcultures and scene, partying's overlap with activism and politics, and the city's DIY, experimentalist spirit are all legacies of the Love Parade, set in motion by that hardy group of 150 promenaders who first brought club culture into the light.

Within a few years of its conception, attendance at
The Love Parade had risen to 150,000

MUNICH

Less DJ Hell than DJ and record label heaven, Munich's underground scene thrives in one of Germany's most conservative regions

With a heritage in club culture that goes back to the days of disco (Giorgio Moroder was a resident here) and later the legendary '90s techno club Ultraschall, it's no wonder Munich has spawned so many talented artists and, particularly, record labels. Compost, Gomma, DJ Hell's Gigolo, through Molten Moods and the Zenker Brothers' Ilian Tape, along with scores of others, have all sought to express Munich's constantly renewing music scene onto vinyl or WAV.

For years, Munich's nightlife revolved around one street, "the Feierbanane" (party banana), but like many cities, rents and pressure from neighbours has started to shift venues away from the centre, with much loved venues like Harry Klein (the original) being replaced by hotels. While Munich has the enlightened licensing laws and free-thinking club scene that typifies Germany, Bavaria is the most conservative of the country's regions.

One exception is BLITZ, found on Museum Island, boasting an international outlook in terms of guests and a music policy that spans house,

techno, disco and even UKG and bass. While crowds and genres bleed into each other across the city, the general musical trend right now is in favour of hard, dark techno, showcased at venues like basement Rote Sonne (on the banana), founded by some of the original Ultraschall crew with guests like Gabber Eleganza, Perc and Minimal Violence.

For a more experimental techno vibe, and reminiscent of the indoor/outdoor experience at Berlin's lamented Spree-side party Bar 25, head to Bahnwärter Thiel, constructed out of shipping containers and decommissioned subway cars around an outdoor pavilion. A space for art installations and even theatre productions, it hosts DJ and live performances by the likes of Franca and Pauli Pocket (both residents of Berlin's Kater Blau), and Shkoon.

And if you're looking for a lower bpm, the petite Goldener Reiter (Golden Jockey) is the spot for disco and house from the laid-back likes of Julie Fleischer or Permanent Vacation's Rosa Red.

Munich is teeming with great bars (this is the home of Oktoberfest, after all), and while they're not concentrated in one area, getting around is easy with the efficient public transport system or, even better, by bike. In summer, getting a permit is tricky for more impromptu outdoor events, but established festivals like the massive Greenfields and Back to the Woods have it covered. The latter is a single day event held in the nearby forest of Garching, with past guests like Bambounou, Honey Dijon and Matrixxman and an afterparty at BLITZ.

◯ RECORD SHOP

Optimal Records
Open, incredibly, since 1982, Munich DJs describe this old-school classic record store as one of the best, not just in the city, but in the world. Selling T-shirts, DVDs and gig tickets alongside vinyl, its knowledgeable staff ensure a selection that ranges widely across genres yet is carefully kept bang up to date.

A retro shot of DJ Hell in 1991

BLITZ's wood-panelled main room, built by David Muallem and the crew

DJ Hell
The international deejay gigolo and on-and-off Munich resident has been on the decks since 1978. He has been front and centre of musical trends since the '90s, from the birth of European techno (releasing his debut track 'My Definition Of House Music' on R&S in 1992), as resident at NYC's Limelight, collaborating with fashion designers from Versace to Hugo Boss and, of course, spearheading the electroclash movement of the late '90s and early '00s by releasing works by Miss Kittin, Tiga et al. Constantly reinventing himself, Hell is one of the most fascinating and influential DJs, A&Rs and figures still active in electronic music today.

Sedef Adasi
Turkish-born BLITZ resident Sedef is a versatile selector whose sets range across electro, house, techno and even disco. After putting her hometown of Augsburg on the map with her HAMAM Nights, inviting heavyweights like DJ Stingray, DMX Krew, Tama Sumo, Boris and Tobias to share the decks with her, she's played across Europe and the UK. She released her debut EP, *Fantasy Zone*, on Public Possession in 2021.

Ilian Tape
Founded by DJ and production Zenker Brothers Dario and Marko, Ilian Tape is built around a core of artists including Andrea, Andrés Zacco, Sciahri, Skee Mask and Stenny, and their diverse taste, a mesh of house, techno, breakbeat, electro, drum'n'bass, and ambient. A favourite with DJs like B.Traits, Midland and fellow Munich local tINI, Ilian Tape's other great admirer is Daniel Avery. "I love the atmosphere of Ilian Tape records; there's a broken beauty to all of them," he says. "The music is intense, but always with a feeling of hope buried inside. It's a special label."

CLUB / EVENT

BLITZ
David Muallem and the BLITZ crew built this two room, 600-cap venue inside the shell of an old museum with meticulous care. From the wooden walls and dancefloor and the custom Void sound system to the inclusive and diverse crowd ("I don't believe in homogenic crowds," says Muallem), and the skilled residents and guests ranging from rRoxymore to Seth Troxler and Dixon, the result is a genuine labour of love.

Greenfields Open Air Festival
This all day festival, held on a racecourse in the east of the city, tends to stick to a formula: the biggest names from the Time Warp / Ibiza end of the techno and tech house spectrum – Amelie Lens, Maceo Plex, Loco Dice, etc. – play all day in the open air, then Sven Väth brings it all home with a headline set. If it ain't broke...

COPEN HAGEN

From Culture Boxes to Island festivals, pump houses to street parties, the home of Coma Club retains the power to surprise

Denmark's capital is a city of paradox. Austere on the outside yet cosy on the inside. Notoriously law abiding (the old cliché about the locals never crossing a deserted street until the lights change holds true), yet home to the outlaw, semi-autonomous commune island of Christiania. Proudly well organised, yet with brutal traffic at times. A place where tourists and expats lament the standoffishness of the locals, yet also home to a warm and welcoming club community.

At the heart of that scene is the long-standing Culture Box, renowned as an institution and refuge for artists and lovers of quality underground electronica since 2005. Half an hour's walk south-west, near the stunning Tivoli Gardens (which itself holds the occasional party), are Pumpehuset and Ved Siden Af. Pumpehuset is a former 19th-century water pumping plant that was transformed into a music venue in the late '80s. The main venue hosts concerts with touring metal and indie bands and live shows from hip-hop stars throughout the year. It also boasts nights like Eclectic Resonance, a trance/techno/progressive party, as well as drum'n'bass/ jungle rave-up Afro Swing, where you might find DJs like the UK's Chimpo and Matra alongside Swedish jungle don Boj Lucki. In the summer, attached garden Byhaven is one of the city's top outdoor party spots. Just down the street is basement joint Ved Siden Af, a venue that takes being a safe space seriously (including Berghain-style stickers on phone lenses) and is the centre of the city's booming bass scene thanks to crews like Bedside – though the downstairs dancefloor does tend to lean into techno most nights.

The entrance to Christiania, Copenhagen's semi-autonomous commune island

Back north-west in the buzzy Nørrebro neighbourhood you'll find the perfectly cubic club Rust, another inclusive spot with a varied schedule. Look out for the Thursday night showcases of up-and-coming local talent and see if you can spot the next MØ or Trentemøller (fun fact: Danish computer keyboards have ø on them, right next to Æ).

On the øther side of the river, things get more industrial at the secluded 350-cap warehouse venue Hangaren, with its booming Funktion-One sound system and local artists like DJ Ibon, home-grown stars like Anastasia Kristensen and international guests like Prins Thomas. Come summertime, the courtyard is the place to be.

And summertime is frankly the best time to visit Copenhagen, not just because for most of the year it has a climate that makes Manchester look positively bright and cheerful, but because that's when the festivals start. These include the massive, five-day, 300 concert, Distortion street party in June, with electronic highlights in 2022 including Four Tet, Octo Octa and Todd Terje, to Journey in Christiania, where Bob Moses and slowthai have starred, to the three-day disco, house and techno fest Karrusel, nestled in an inner city woodland grove.

Courtesy, raised in Copenhagen, was formerly part of the city's Apeiron crew of DJs and artists

DJS / LABEL

Kølsch
Born in a commune on the outlaw island of Christiania, the half-Irish committed hat wearer Rune Reilly Kölsch was already a well respected behind-the-scenes producer (as Rune RK and Artificial Funk) before he decided to turn his hand to creating timeless anthems like 'Der Alte' and 'Grey'. He has become one of the few DJs who can hold any crowd, from tens of thousands at a festival to a few hundred in a basement, in the palm of his hand from start to finish.

Courtesy
When *Mixmag* wanted to write a lengthy feature article about Courtesy a few years ago, she instead asked to turn the spotlight on the struggles and activism at Tblisi's Bassiani club. Greenland-born and Copenhagen-raised (she was formerly part of the city's Apeiron crew of DJs and artists with Sara Svanholm, Simone Øster and Scottish export Emma Blake) her DJ sets and production show the same generosity of spirit, boldly mixing pitched down techno, trance, and references from the rave continuum with striking melodies and a dark playfulness.

In My Room
Essentially just a label for Trentemøller to release his own music, and very occasionally friends like Dorit Chrysler and Tom Bertelsen, In My Room is nevertheless a great place to start exploring the work of one of Copenhagen's most interesting artists of the past decade, a man who was making 'dark disco' well before the genre had been coined.

CLUB / EVENT

Culture Box
Actually two boxes in one: Red box (a subterranean, low ceilinged bunker for house and disco) and Black Box (big guests from Ellen Allien to Maribou State), linked by a warren of tunnels. Each one has a custom sound system, adding to Culture Box's rep as the standard-bearer of the club scene in Copenhagen through good times and bad, often four nights a week. As Kompakt's Michael Mayer says, "They've run a strict 'no compromise' policy since 2005 and the club is still on fire. It's one of those clubs where you instantly feel at home."

Kune
Held on Ungdomsøen ('youth island') between Denmark and Sweden, KUNE, named after the esperanto word for 'together', launched in 2019. Far from being a Girl Guides event, or indeed any kind of cult, KUNE is a four-day house, techno and ambient festival with a strong arts focus and a line-up that includes DJs like Culture Box resident MHM One and local hero Tight Cherry.

Guy J at Culture Box

O RECORD SHOP

313vinyl_collective
This second-hand vinyl store by the railway tracks specialises in classic Detroit techno and Chicago house, with a large catalogue from revered labels like Transmat, KMS, Underground Resistance, Metroplex, Axis, Synewave, Plus 8, Dance Mania, Trax and Fragile. 313 is, of course, the area code for Detroit.

COMA CLUB

In the 1980s, Kenneth Bager was resident DJ at Daddys, a pop art palace that had, for years, been the hottest discotheque in the country. But there was a sense that nightlife could mean something more. "We thought it was quite boring," says Coma co-founder Jack Rothe. "The night seemed to get better the later you went out; we hated that, why shouldn't it be great from the beginning?" Trips to Ibiza, London and across Europe had convinced them that the city, and Denmark, needed more action. Jack and Kenneth put on a party, Amok, in 1986 in an old cinema and let their imaginations run riot. The door staff were dressed as characters from *A Clockwork Orange*. There was a boxing ring on the main dance floor with local fighters knocking lumps out of each other all night (except for a short interval where a heavy metal band took over). Blow-up dolls were hung from the ceiling. The restrooms were filled with children's toys. Silhouetted behind screens on scaffolding were X-rated local 'performers'. The cinema screen showed an old Danish comedy classic, upside down and backwards. Fancy dress was mandatory. And the dancefloor was filled with popcorn. The madness, creativity and flair for the unexpected would set the tone for the next 25 years.

The first Coma party proper took place in August 1988, starting in an old ballroom called the Lorry, and moving years later to unexpected venues from the National Museum to the famous Tivoli Gardens and even an old customs house by the harbour. It brought the new wave of house music and the spirit of the acid house scene – at that time spreading across Europe from Ibiza like smiley faced wildfire – to Denmark for the first time. But it also echoed the spirit of the New York scene that Kenneth and his friends had read so much about but never experienced: the flamboyance of the Limelight club kids in New York and the strict door policy of Steve Rubell at Studio 54. Coma introduced rules to make sure that people were there for the right reasons: fancy, outrageous dress was an entry requirement and tickets were to be bought in advance to start the party in people's heads weeks before the event. And the club held up its end of the bargain, always surprising and delighting the faithful with new feats of imagination, bringing international DJs and acts to Copenhagen for the first time: Red Alert, Paul Oakenfold, Bomb the Bass, Coldcut and Lisa Stansfield,

Todd Terry. The combination of anything-goes partying, incredible costumes and glamorous, sexy people saw the club on the country's news and in the papers – even in the national news on TV. Soon, provincial Danish towns were throwing their own 'Coma' nights. In June '89, aware of the commercial monster they had created, they shut the party down.

It was Copenhagen's most anticipated party of the new millennium when Coma returned in 2004. Since then, they have stayed true to the club's principles while always seeking to outdo themselves, putting on nights themed around Robin Hood or sausages, and parties in the National Museum where revellers were greeted on the door by strobe-lit butchers chopping up meat and real blood drinks for sale at the bar. These days, Coma hold three parties a year in the city, and tickets never take more than minutes to sellout. Coma may now almost be a national treasure, but each night retains the power to surprise and thrill.

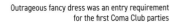

Outrageous fancy dress was an entry requirement
for the first Coma Club parties

WARSAW

Dancers at Jasna 1, a proudly LGBTQ+ space

The punky, politically active club culture of Poland's capital fires a scene that's among the strongest in Europe

An unexpectedly stunning city where art nouveau neighbourhoods nestle up against Soviet era brutalism, packed with bars and restaurants (including continent-leading vegan cuisine), Warsaw is an oft-overlooked tourist gem – especially for electronic music fans.

The scene here can trace its beginnings to a single event. This first acid house party in Warsaw took place in April 1991 in a derelict former bath house in Rutkowskiego street. This party was thrown by Tomek Hornung, who had lived in London during the acid house eruption and was visiting Warsaw with his decks and mixer to team up with Dariusz "Skandal" Hajn from the famous Polish punk band Dezerter. This punk beginning set the template for the politically-involved ethos of much of Warsaw's club culture, as well as its deep love for techno (traditionally other Polish cities like Woj and Krakow have been far more inclined to breakbeats than the capital).

Today, the main clubs in Warsaw can all be found in the city centre and well within walking distance of each other. Visiting several in a night is pretty standard, helped by low entrance fees and none of them closing before 7am (some are open even later into the morning). Luzztro is the most renowned of the afterhours. Started in 2003 by a bunch of friends who met through the techno scene, the 300-cap steel lined cube avoids international bookings, prioritising local talent like Truant and Kalicky. Nearby, the larger Smolna, housed in a three-storey tenement building, is renowned for bringing international techno and tech house DJs to the city; the likes of Steffi, Bjarki

⦿ RECORD SHOP

Side One
Despite its small size, this much loved record store in the city centre overflows (literally) with new and second-hand vinyl. Highly prized by the city's DJs and artists, it's not unusual to find local producers discussing remixes and tech, having wandered in with a couple of beers in hand (it's BYOB).

and Shlømo. Meanwhile, Jasna 1 has been at the centre of a slight house renaissance lately, at least in one of its two rooms, thanks to crews like Move Mózg collective and a lovingly inclusive and easygoing vibe. Outside the city centre, the Praga area is known for its post-industrial chic, bars and cafés.

Besides the three main clubs there's also been a big post-lockdown influx of new crews and DJs organising parties, such as the Trainspotting techno events held in a warehouse near the old train station, collectives like queer facing Glitter Confusion, Splot Słoneczny (organic house sounds), and Aurora Station (progressive-house) in outdoor summertime venue Lunapark. Meanwhile, the anonymous DJ and party collective Wixapol have led a renaissance of gabber and hardcore, not just in Warsaw but across the country and indeed Europe, building a scene with its own fashion aesthetic and even its own rave slang; a kind of Polish rave Polari.

Another crew at the centre of Poland's scene for two decades is Warsaw's Instytut. Founded by Iwona Korzybska, Joanna Wielkopolan and Gerhard Derksen, inspired by events like Awakenings and Dekmantel in Amsterdam, the trio have launched events across the city and beyond. Let's Plant a Techno Forest was an event in Stefanów, a village south-east of Warsaw, where attendees – you guessed it – planted saplings by day and danced to techno at night. They are also responsible for the Instytut Festival, a three-day event set in the ruins of a 19th-century fortress in the centre of the country with acts like Nina Kraviz, Dax J, Kobosil and Random, and of course their parties in the monumental Institute of Power Engineering building on the outskirts of the city.

Warsaw's club scene has been at the forefront of support for the LGBTQ+ and migrant community in the country and the resistance against creeping religious populism (notably taking to the city's streets for the Women's Strike protests in 2020). It has also been deeply involved in the entire country's heroic support for its neighbour Ukraine, from fundraising to venues throwing their doors open for transiting refugees.

DJS / LABEL

VTSS
Cutting her DJ teeth initially with the Wixapol crew and as a resident at Jasna 1, VTSS has become known for her brand of mixing hard-hitting techno with a light, fun attitude. It's dynamic, daring and often tongue-in-cheek, taking cues from the heady days of '90s dance music culture. Since her third release *Identity Process* landed on Repitch, she's seen her profile skyrocket with regular spots at Berghain, plus everyone from Blawan to Rebekah dropping her tunes on the regular.

Jurek Przezdziecki
A stalwart of the Polish scene for years – releasing everything from techno on Cocoon to psytrance to avant-garde jazz under a variety of aliases including Epi Centrum – Przezdziecki made an unexpected connection with Siberian powerhouse Nina Kraviz when she played five of his obscure psytrance records in a typically deep digging closing set at 2021's Exit festival. The day Przezdziecki was alerted to it, she got in touch about a remix for her TRIP label.

U Know Me Records
Born out of JuNouMi Records, formed in 2002 by a crew of Polish hip hop fanatics, U Know Me debuted in 2010 with a groundbreaking release from one man beat factory and sonic world builder Teielte and hasn't looked back since. Styles range far and wide across the electronic landscape, from the dubby post-rave of Janka to a Polish take on UKG from TVB.

CLUB / CREW

barStudio
This theatre bar in the Palace of Culture and Science is at the centre of Warsaw's club culture. With the bar plastered with posters for parties and events, DJs regularly playing in the courtyard outside, and vinyl fairs, it is also where the activist wing of the scene tend to meet to organise.

Instytut
The Instytut crew have been holding bi-annual events in the colossal concrete central structure (think Chernobyl school of architecture) of the Instytut Energetyki on and off since 2000, when Claude Young headlined the first party. In one of the most spectacular settings for a rave-up in Europe, they've since hosted everyone from Chris Liebing and Luke Slater to The Advent and Marcel Dettmann.

An Instytut party in the phenomenal industrial setting of the Insitute of Power Engineering

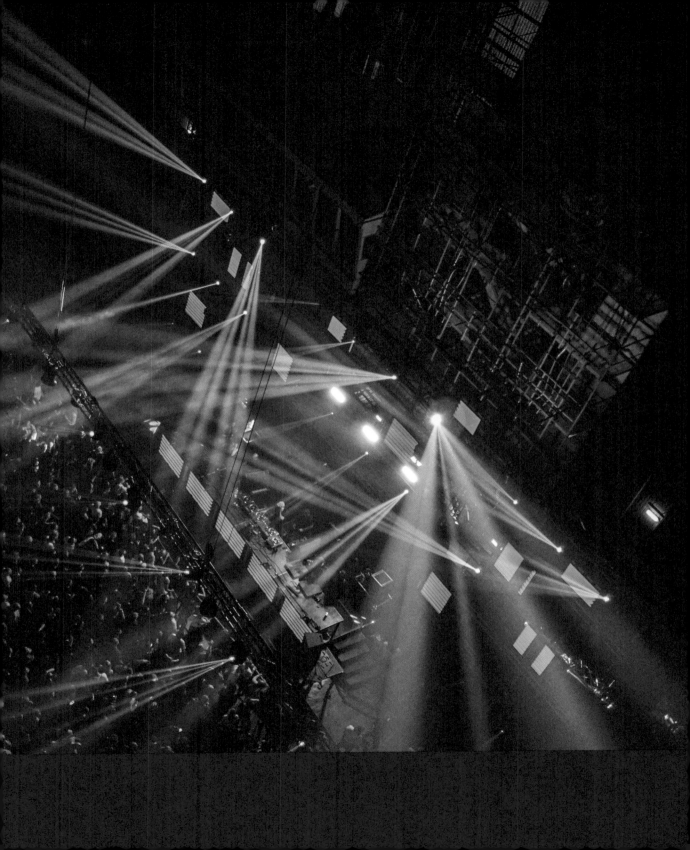

BEL GRA DE

Taxis are scarce but great nights out are plentiful in Serbia's hard-partying capital

Belgrade's club scene is booming. Dating back to the '90s, it hunkered down during the Yugoslavian war, was fuelled by the sense of liberation after the resignation of President Milošević in 2000, and was catalysed by the rise of the EXIT festival in Novi Sad to the north of the capital at the same time.

A focal point of the EXIT crew's citywide No Sleep Festival, Hangar is exactly as it sounds: a colossal industrial venue of steel balconies and vast space that's the perfect backdrop for the huge techno names that the festival brings to the city in April, from Nina Kraviz to DVS1 and DJ Bone. It's also capable of surprising transformation: a recent gig with Folamour saw the LEDs stripped out in favour of an intimate, vintage vibe, with a cascade of disco balls and warm lighting. Open at least once a month for something big, it's at the epic end of Belgrade's event scale.

The renowned Drugstore club is hardly more conventional. Based in a converted slaughterhouse with a raw, none-more-industrial feel that some compare to the OG techno scene in '90s Berlin, it attracts names like Nastia, Legowelt and Shlømo, alongside Serbian DJs and crews, and even the occasional indie gig or live show.

And the list goes on: from the perfectly formed DOT, punching well above its 200 capacity with a focus on the melodic side of house and techno, to the nomadic Blender parties, mixing up styles and genres, the city has a lot to offer. Techno has always been the bedrock of Belgrade's scene: "We like it banging," says DJ Miroslav Miletić, "but house has never left the building, and disco is coming back." 20/44 and the yearly Matinée Fest (headlined by Honey Dijon in 2021) fly the house flag. On the slopes of the medieval fortress of Kalemegdan sits Barutana, an outdoor summer venue hosting psytrance parties.

While it is common to visit multiple clubs in one night, they are spread out across the city, and a recent and chronic shortage of taxis due to economic pressures (and a drought of drivers) means it's crucial to do your homework and plan your route beforehand. As is planning your afterparty. Venues like the KPTM club (a courtyard-style space often open from the night before until 2pm the next day) and half are an oasis for the bed-shy. Look out for daily updates on the club social media to keep your finger on the fast moving scene. Before the club (or clubs), the Dorćol neighbourhood in the Old City is home to places like Cetinjska 15, a key pre-club hangout with numerous bars ranging from the stylish 808 and LIFT, to ersatz 'backyard' boozers. Savamala, by the Brankov Bridge, is another buzzing neighbourhood and home to house music venue Culture Centre Grad. Though not a huge tourist destination, and definitely retaining a bit of an outlaw vibe, people on the club scene are warm, friendly and hospitable: just try to keep up.

Marko Nastić

At the age of 18, Nastic formed a crew called Teenage Techno Punks, throwing underground free techno parties that remain an urban legend in Belgrade today. "We were really frightened that we were going to be bombed," Nastic says. "There were periods where we couldn't go out on the streets at night, so we made parties during the day." Once the war stuttered to an end at the turn of the century, Nastic's career quickly gained momentum, and bookings came in from Europe, then America, then all over the world. He runs three labels and has been a resident at EXIT for more than 10 years.

Tijana T

One of the country's proudest DJ exports, Tijana Todorovic began as a journalist, broadcaster and TV presenter covering the Belgrade music scene before her international profile took off in the early 2010s. Having played everywhere from Berghain and fabric to Amnesia and Bassiani, her selection is wide-ranging, though the acid squiggle of a 303 is never very far away.

CLUB / EVENT

Klub 20/44

Probably Belgrade's coolest spot right now, this club, set on a sprawling river barge (or 'splav'), has been repping Belgrade's house scene ever since opening in 2009. It played a formative role in Tijana's T's breakout and is now home to more up-and-coming local talent, as well as guests like Hunnee, Palms Trax and Hodge.

No Sleep

If you can only make one weekend in Belgrade, make it early April, when EXIT offshoot No Sleep takes over the Hangar and other venues in the city and the already fevered nightlife in Belgrade raises its game even further. Local luminaries like Tijana T and Kristijan Molnar line up alongside guests from DJ Tennis to Stephan Bodzin.

O RECORD SHOP

Yugovinyl

Electronic music isn't the prime focus of the biggest record shop in Serbia. Its collection of rare, second-hand Yugoslavian era punk and alternative music attracts people from all over the world. But it does have a decent selection, outdoor seating, and the potential for hours of crate digging.

Klub 20/44 has been at the centre of Belgrade's house scene since 2009

EXIT

In the year 2000, Serbia was still mired in the conflict of the Yugoslav wars. Beginning when the different Balkan nations in the Yugoslav republic sought to assert their independence after the fall of the Soviet Union, the wars unleashed deep-rooted ethnic enmities, horrific atrocities and – in Serbia – devastating NATO bombing. It was also still ruled by the same corrupt, repressive and warmongering regime, one headed by President Slobodan Milošević.

The first EXIT Festival came as a reaction to a law Milošević passed in 1998 that banned freedom of speech among universities. In the campus town of Novi Sad, students and activists erected stages between the University and the Danube for a 100-day protest against the Milošević regime, camouflaged as an event to get young people more interested in politics. Alongside punk bands, sound systems and speeches, the protest organisers aired the regime's atrocities on a giant TV screen and called for an "Exit out of 10 years of madness."

"EXIT Festival was the first place in the Balkans... where young people and different nations, religions and political convictions met for the first time," says Rastko Andrić, EXIT's Programme and Booking Manager, who was there. The festival/protest didn't just help to mobilise the youth of the country against the regime (and help the rest of the population articulate their own feelings of nausea and exhaustion with the country's direction); it pointed to another vision for the country to unite behind.

And a few days after the festival finished, the presidential elections began, and Milošević was ousted (he'd die in 2006 while on trial for war crimes in The Hague). The following year, EXIT moved into the breathtaking Petrovaradin fortress across the river, its unique permanent home (archaeologists are still exploring 16km of tunnels, four storeys deep, beneath the structure). And over twenty years later it's been visited by millions of people from Serbia, Europe and far beyond, revamping the image of the country, inspiring events across the region from Sziget Festival in Hungary to Neversea in Romania, and also lighting the creative spark for generations of Serbian musicians, artists, DJs and creatives.

Serbian DJ and producer Sladjana Cirjak aka Sugar Lobby first experienced dance music at EXIT Festival when she was 16 years old. "I never stopped after that," she says. "I realised through EXIT that electronic music was my future. The people were so connected. Before, during the problems, the music scene wasn't open to electronic music. But EXIT brought big-name artists and DJs into Serbia. For me, it was like another world."

EXIT has been headlined by everyone from Sepultura to Lauryn Hill to the Arctic Monkeys and Grace Jones, without losing either its electronic edge or its commitment to wider social aims. Their initiative Youth Heroes funds exceptional young Serbians who are keen to contribute to society through university, and in 2019 the team launched the Green R:evolution, a mass reforestation project with the aim of planting one million trees in Serbia alone. "In 2020 we planted around thirteen thousand oak trees in Novi Sad," says Head of Booking Miroslav Miletić. "EXIT was, and still is, a movement for freedom – and we'll continue to remind people of the negative impact of climate change and educate them on how to reverse it."

Did a music festival really bring down a government? EXIT certainly played its part. And they're not finished yet.

The ruined battlements of the fortress at EXIT alive with ravers

CROATIAN RIVIERA

101 festivals transform the Dalmatian Coast each Summer in the new epicentre of outdoor electronic music culture

The unexpected rise of Croatia's Adriatic coast to become an electronic festival hotspot began in the 1990s with a rave in Zagreb called Future Shock. 15,000 people attended each of the 1994-1996 (revived in 2001) events, which bristled with hardcore, trance and techno. But connecting the idea of these large scale events to the beautiful coastal regions with their sandy beaches, limestone smugglers' coves and outdoor disco-style venues and beach shacks was done by a pair of holidaying British promoters and their families when they launched the 300-strong Garden festival in an abandoned nightclub in Petrcane in 2005.

The old sound systems and free parties had been exploring the idea of setting up events in Europe's far-flung locations for decades. Clubbers from all over Europe were used to descending on Ibiza every summer, or even to cities for things like Berlin's Love Parade, but the idea of going overseas specifically for a festival, and an electronic music festival at that, was a new concept for many. Fortunately, Croatia was the perfect setting. The infrastructure – outdoor venues, hotels and restaurants, bars, even party boats – may have been a little down at heel (especially given the ravages of war a decade earlier), but it was there. The authorities were mostly accommodating. Local businesses were thrilled. The scenery and climate are stunning. Prices were cheap and budget airlines were offering routes. Word got around and nowadays, Croatia is the first name in overseas festivals, especially for British clubbers.

Zrće beach in particular has transformed itself around the new festival and music demographic. A strip of huge seafront outdoor clubs on a sheltered pebble beach on Pag Island, the original is Kalypso, over 30 years in situ and these days a huge open air dancefloor surrounded by bars and balconies and platforms. Next door are Aquarius, Papaya, with its two pools and stunning elevated views, and the newest addition, Noa, built on a series of islands with 11 bars, multiple dancefloors and space for 3,000 partygoers. The Zrće beach hosts festivals like Fresh Island, three days of hip-hop and r'n'b with the likes of DJ Semtex and Skillibeng in June, as well as Hideout in July, five days of pool, boat, and afterparties with 100+ DJs (think a bass driven list including Andy C, CamelPhat, Chase & Status, FISHER, Gorgon City, Hannah Wants, Holy Goof, Jamie Jones, Hot Since 82, Skream, and Artwork). Zrće is also the home of Sonus, run by the techno loving crew behind Time Warp in Mannheim and featuring DJs like Amelie Lens, Carl Cox, Chris Liebing, Dixon, Loco Dice, Monika Kruse and Seth Troxler.

Another festival hotspot is The Garden resort, set in its own bay, a natural amphitheatre near the town of Tisno. A former holiday camp for workers of the state oil company, this was where that pioneering Garden festival moved a few years later when 3,500 ravers got a bit too much for the sleepy fishing village of Petrcane. Tisno – dreamier, more rural and boutique than Zrce – is home to events like Garden festival's successor, Love International, and SuncéBeat, a full week of quality underground house, disco, techno, soul, r'n'b and funk, who were the first to bring deep house titan Larry Heard to the Garden, the first to invite Berlin powerhouse Prosumer to spin, and the first Croatian festival to secure a date with the semi-mythical DJ Harvey, plus other legends such as DJ Jazzy Jeff and Black Coffee. The Garden is also the location for Dimensions, perhaps Croatia's most cutting edge line-up featuring acts in 2022 like Sherelle, Eris Drew b2b Octo Octa, Helena Hauff b2b DJ Stingray 313, Tama Sumo, LSDXOXO and Mor Elian.

While the local authorities have adjusted to coexist with a huge festival scene (the police are no longer sectioning people they find overdoing ketamine to the local psychiatric hospital, a harrowing yet somehow hilarious feature of some of those early parties), there's still little Croatian involvement in the festivals mentioned as punters or as DJs. But hopefully that will evolve, and meanwhile electronic music has had a positive impact on the local economy. This seasonal, transplanted scene has certainly turned the sleepy Dalmatian coast into a dance music hot capital.

DJ

Maja Pa
Part of the Zagreb based bRAVE crew – together with Ikonal and Le Chocolat Noir – Maya Pavlovic's techno meets EBM meets dark electro sets are a feature of the cooler end of the Croatian festival scene. A regular at Dekmantel Selectors, Dimensions and Love International, off season she plays across the Balkans and beyond at clubs like Berlin's Tresor.

EVENTS

Love International
Probably the vibiest, most inclusive and friendliest of all the Croatian festivals, Love International at the Garden is built around a warm communion between the crowd and DJs like Anz, Crazy P Soundsystem, DJ Tennis, Gerd Janson, Midland, Saoirse, and Roman Flügel.

Dekmantel Selectors
Another Garden event, this has the kind of musical breadth and depth that Dekmantel events across the world have become known for; names like Kode9 rubbing shoulders with Shanti Celeste, Special Request and Teki Latex. Look out for label-run boat parties, too, with the likes of Clone and Rush Hour.

Love International attracts the biggest names in electronic music, from Gerd Janson to Peggy Gou (pictured)

165

TBILISI

<u>Perhaps no city in the world has a club culture that finds itself
on the front line of the actual culture wars quite like Tbilisi</u>

The picturesque Georgian capital was always a popular tourist destination for those behind the iron curtain (possibly helped by the fact that Stalin grew up here). Tbilisi has a rich history that goes back to the days when it was a key stopping point on the Silk Road from China to Europe. Its architecture takes in the narrow streets and pastel buildings of the old town of Kala, the bulbous spires of Orthodox Churches, grand Art Nouveau hotels and Soviet brutalism, all in the shadow of the 4th-century Narikala Fortress. And since the breakup of the Soviet Union and Georgia's independence, and after the war of 2008, Tbilisi has in turn become a destination for visitors around the world drawn to its sights, history, great food and wine, and unique character.

With new visitors and a new spirit of liberation, the city's club scene also began to take shape, with venues like the now world-famous Bassiani attracting adventurous underground DJs from across Europe in the 2010s and becoming a focal point for the city's outsider, creative and queer communities. This didn't make everyone happy. Georgia's blossoming club culture is in direct conflict with its 90 per cent Orthodox Christian population, many of whom are strongly against alternative culture and do not believe in equal rights for the LGBTQ+ community. "There's still a Soviet mentality [in Georgia]," says local DJ Sandro Mezurnishvili. The 'shadow of the bear' hasn't helped either: "Russia has acquired 20 per cent of our territory and uses fake news and propaganda to create conflict."

The empire struck back on 12 May 2018 with raids on Bassiani and Cafe Gallery, two of the city's major clubs. The pretext for the raids by Georgia's special forces was that they were a strike against drug dealers in the wake of five drug-related deaths in the city. That pretext was swiftly debunked: eight drug dealers were arrested that evening, but the arrests had been made in the streets three hours prior to the raids. It later emerged that the total value of drugs seized in the eight arrests was 2,000 GEL – around £550 or $650 –

Punters queueing outside Bassiani. Photograph by George Nebieridze.

and none of the five deaths were connected to any club. The action was quickly interpreted by many involved in the city's club scene as a show of intimidation against the values of freedom, liberalism and tolerance that Tbilisi's clubs had come to represent – driven by the Russian-influenced church and press. A campaign of harassment against the local scene followed. On one occasion, a group of female DJs returning to Tbilisi from Berlin were stopped, detained and searched without a warrant, even being taken to hospital for MRI scans to try to find non-existent drugs hidden in their bodies.

Unbowed and unbroken, the city's scene has fought back, with a unity that would be inconceivable in many other places. "Never in our wildest dreams did we think they would do this," says Alexander Gabrichidze, manager of the KHIDI club, as he describes his experience on May 12. "We stopped the music immediately and asked everyone to come with us to Bassiani to support them." The scene here is powered by righteous passion. While drug laws are incredibly harsh and the fight to preserve the city's nightlife continues, this is a stunning destination with an incredible club community. Besides Bassiani and KHIDI, look out for summer events at Mtatsminda Park by the television broadcast tower.

Dancers at KHIDI

Natalie Beridze

At the forefront of Tbilisi's explosive arts scene since the mid-'90s, when she became a member of Georgia's first multimedia collective, Natalie's other-worldly, haunting electronica was snapped up by labels early in her career. Berlin-based WMF Records offered her a contract in 2002, and she's since released over 26 albums and EPs. Titles such as *What About Things Like Bullets, Mapping Debris* and *Love is Winning* make clear her political beliefs.

Berika

Born and raised in the city, Irakli Berikashvili, aka Berika, makes fast, contagious dance tracks,though ICONTRAX, the label he heads, focuses on deep house, techno and ambient. Playing across every club in the city, he's a believer in electronic music's potential to build a new and liberated Georgia. "What most musicians here are trying to do is create a cultural platform," he says. "It doesn't matter if we're experimental, techno, house – clubs are promoting local music and representing us to others."

CLUBS

KHIDI

This 1,200 cap venue, whose name means 'the bridge' in Georgian, is actually built into the riverside beneath one of the main bridges across the Mtkvari. It's a bunker style venue with a main floor dedicated to techno, and more eclectic sounds in the second room. Like most Tbilisi venues, it's also used for galleries, exhibitions and all kinds of artistic endeavours by day.

Bassiani

Despite its unlikely location inside the innards of a football stadium, Bassiani is Georgia's most legendary club and the focus of its underground community. Regularly visited by international DJs from Courtesy to Marcel Dettmann, alongside talented residents like Zitto and HVL, the music is techno, the atmosphere is intense, and the club holds 1,200 people.

Natalie Beridze has been at the forefront of Georgia's art scene since the 1990s. Photograph by George Nebieridze.

● RECORD SHOP

Vodkast

Beginning in 2010 as a podcast mix series, Vodkast opened as a record store five years later by the banks of the Mtkvari. Tbilisi's first electronic record shop, it soon became a hangout for the local DJ community, and launched a record label. Look out for their occasional in-store sessions.

Chapter 4

AFRICA & THE MIDDLE EAST

Kampala

Johannesburg

Tel Aviv-Y

nasburg

TUNIS

It's still early days for the Tunis club scene, but a new generation of harder, faster artists and crews is starting to show its potential

The lockdown of Tunis's clubs during the pandemic accelerated the rave scene in and around the city. Several collectives have had such an impact with their events that they're now looking beyond the model of hiring a house or villa outside Tunis for a pseudo-private party and into bigger and more ambitious events, as well as heading back into the city to bring new sounds to the clubs. Downtown Vibes (the mastermind behind the Secret Vibes parties), XPAM (a group of 20-somethings pushing industrial techno, who have secured a bunker-style venue in the city), and Vince City (who rep the melodic side of house and techno) are just a few examples. Many of the collectives are non-profit, ploughing whatever they earn back into the next party.

This is an exciting but relatively fledgling scene, with supportive and committed crowds who are used to seeing DJs improve exponentially from week to week. It can also be a little cliquey, with the same DJs tending to dominate at the expense of talent breaking through. But given that many venues don't even have their own decks and equipment (in many cases the DJ has to hire them out of their fee or split the door take to cover the expense), it's definitely still early days.

In the city, the clubbing action is concentrated in Gammarth, a tourist and hotel neighbourhood by the shores of the Mediterranean, compact and easily navigable by foot. Two venue complexes

lead the underground scene: Habibi Tunis, 117 Gammarth and the chilled out beachfront bar Yuka are all interconnected, as are the Basement Club and Gingembre a few minutes walk away. Downtown you'll find the Marengo, a converted darkroom. Clubs are open from 8pm and are more expensive to enter after midnight, and Tunis's thrifty young clubbers tend to take advantage of early bird ticket offers and discounts to make their hard-earned cash go further. Alcohol is perfectly legal here (look out for local beer Celtia). Taxis are the main way of getting around – the locals use a taxi collective to pare fares down to pennies – but stay near the Gammarth and you can walk everywhere. While certain venues like Gingembre, for example, have a reputation for being LGBTQ+ friendly, bear in mind that it's all relative and attitudes may not be as open as in European or North American cities.

The biggest recent change in Tunis's music scene has been the move away from the house sound that dominated here for years towards industrial, minimal and even hardcore techno. DJs like Fatysh will drop a six-hour hardcore set at XPAM's warehouse without blinking, while OA is another name to watch for industrial vibes. Look out for the long-running Fabrika festival, which brings the biggest names in Minimal techno (most recently Romanian titans Rhadoo and Raresh) to Tunis – and of course the return of the incredible Les Dunes Electronique.

XPAM's warehouse, home to the collective's industrial techno parties

PRODUCER / DJ / LABEL

Ahmed Mecnun
Tunisia's most famous production talent, and perhaps its most prolific. Creating techno and tech house and collaborating with a host of overseas producers, his records have found favour with everyone from Marco Carola, Nicole Moudaber and Paco Osuna among others.

SARLA
One of few female DJs in what's still a male dominated scene, XPAM resident SARLA stands out for her ability to weave EBM, acid and other genres within an industrial techno framework to create something that's at once banging yet hypnotic.

Are You Alien
Founded by Tunis DJ and producer HearThuG and co-owned by vocalist Fig Republic and fellow DJ and producer Emine, Are You Alien specialises in acid house and techno sounds, while DJs from its stable are hugely active in the local scene – there will always be at least one of them playing Tunis every week.

CLUB

Basement
Tunis's most ambitious club in terms of booking DJs from outside the city, the 800-capacity Basement will tend to have guests from the global underground about twice a month: names like France's Traumer or Italy's Mind Against, as well as hosting local collectives like Downtown Vibes.

O RECORD SHOP

Eddisco
Tunis is a crate digger's paradise, home to dusty record shops full of gems from French and Arabic pop music and oddities from across the Mediterranean. But the tiny Eddisco, run by the Downtown Vibes crew, is a rare spot for electronic music, with pop art-painted walls and a selection ranging across house, techno and hip-hop to jazz, disco and obscure Tunisian and Arabic records. By appointment only, but a great gateway to the scene.

LES DUNES ELECTRONIQUE

The idea to hold a festival on the desert site used as a backdrop for the Tatooine scenes in the original *Star Wars* trilogy came to Matthieu Corosine and his partner in Panda Events, Benoit Geli, when they met the owners of a Tunisian hotel at a beach festival in Nice. Invited to celebrate the end of the season at the hotel, a trip to the 'Mos Espa' site had them struck with its potential. That trip was in 2011, in the aftermath of the Arab Spring,which had seen the Tunisian people rise up against the country's dictatorship The political situation wasn't stable enough for the first festival until 2014, says Matthieu. But by that time they had another problem: "40 per cent of the set was covered in sand! The dunes here can reclaim a site this size in three weeks." Despite surviving four decades (since the filming of *Star Wars*), the site is a fragile one – "it's made out of nothing". A Kickstarter project and an invitation to fans to help rehabilitate the site, saw it returned to its current condition, and its status as a key tourist destination in this part of the world.

Happily, that 2014 debut coincided with Tunisia confirming its democratic constitution, and this boutique festival in the desert became a focal point for celebration, with over 7,000 people (6,000 more than the original festival was planned for) making the journey to celebrate 'the new Tunisia'. The connections with local partners, especially the tourist board, are key in making Les Dunes Electroniques possible, says Mattheiu: "they know the tricks and they know how to not hurt the environment"). A chance meeting with the Minister of Tourism on that first trip to Nefta began a partnership that sees the authorities help with everything, from security and press arrangements to convincing the national airline to put on more flights to nearby Tozeur.

The main part of the festival is set up around the outside of the Mos Espa set itself, the bulk of which is open only to certain ticket holders and artists. Some of the buildings are carpeted with blankets and the odd table to create perhaps the most picturesque green rooms of all time. At night, it's lit up with coloured floodlights which make those iconic silhouettes stand out even more. Facing outwards at each end are two stages: 'Sunset' and 'Sunrise' (named for the direction they face, they're both open straight through for the 30-hour duration of the event, from Saturday afternoon to Sunday night). A long VIP tent runs alongside the 'village', lined with rugs and dotted with low couches, and there's an indoor arena on the outer rim of the site. Most of the action takes place in front of the stages and around the edge, and beyond the fence during the day roam camels led by cheeky youths insistently offering rides and souvenir selfies at a price to those scrambling over the dunes. The crowd (usually far more manageable than at that bumper first event) tends to be mostly Tunisian, with many from Tunis on what might be their own first trip to the desert southlands. 2019's line-up included a mix of Tunisian artists like Hazem Berrebah and Noy Ära alongside overseas names like Stimming and Apollonia.

A seven-hour car journey from Tunis, the trip is worth every moment: the desert is beautiful, and partying for a weekend among domes and structures oddly familiar from childhood is an utterly unique experience.

The site of Les Dunes Electronique will be familiar to Star Wars fans

KAM PALA

Grab a boda boda and brace for the weekend in K'La, where nightlife is far from an exact science

Nightlife in Kampala (K'la to the locals) is a moveable feast, with DJs and nights often switching venues and locations, but there's method to the madness. The scene here runs on word of mouth -- seek out local knowledge rather than Google. Easing you into the week is 'band' – a type of chilled live music night that's become very à la mode post-COVID – while some of the liveliest DJ sets can be heard mid-week in the unlikeliest of places, like Kyadondo Rugby Club in Lugogo on a Tuesday and Bukoto's Panamera on Wednesdays. Beginning on Monday and ending on Sunday, kibaala (Luganda for the bar scene) takes centre stage. *Kibaala* includes everything from the plush, cosmopolitan lounges found on the affluent strips of Bugolobi and Kololo to the muchomo joints or *kafunda* in Ntinda and Kabalagala – roadside bars serving roasted meats and the most lethal of local brews, frequented by the city's high rollers and average Joes alike.

Uganda is a dancing nation. On any given night out in K'la, you can expect to hear a smorgasbord of sounds: from the Afrobeats and Afropop native to West Africa to South Africa's house music genre of the moment: amapiano, championed worldwide by acts like the Major League DJz and Kamo Mphela. Coming in at a close second is the nation's own homemade brew of dancehall-reggaeton fusion sounds, as well as heavy doses of dance music from neighbouring Congo. As with many a postcolonial city, it's rare to find a DJ playing what is deemed locally as *mzungu* or 'European' music, and a request to do so will likely be met with a blank stare.

Come the weekend, students from the poky dorms of Makerere University and dingy hostels of Wandegeya flock to the more conventional nightclub experiences found at GUVNOR and Illusion. A climate as warm as Uganda's, however, calls for al fresco drinking. Spots like H2O Lounge, La Paroni's, EXO and L'a Venti provide strong booze, good food, great music and shisha.

Boda bodas (motorcycle taxis) are an essential mode of transport, especially for clubbers. The nature of bar hopping – which this speedy taxi service facilitates – gave rise to the global smash hit and de facto national anthem, 'Parte After Parte', by Ugandan rapper BigTril. Cheap and easy, boda bodas are a perfect – albeit hair-raising – way to zip around town, avoiding the one thing that Kampalans dread most: jam.

On Saturdays, many Kampalans trade the hustle and bustle of the city for the unique oasis of neighbouring Entebbe, where beautiful beaches line the shores of Lake Victoria. Back in the capital, the party is in full swing come evening, especially in neighbourhoods like Acacia Avenue and Bandali Rise. The Avenue specialises in sophisticated lounges for the leisurely 'turn up', often with dazzling panoramic views of the city: check out Kush, Cielo, Riders, and Sky Lounge. Bandali Rise is home to venues like vault UG, Karibu and Mango Grove as well as The Alchemist, Caliente and Thrones – considered the trifecta of club hopping in K'la. Across all of these clubs you'll hear a pan-African mix of Ugandan dancehall and reggaeton, Nigerian pop, Congolese Soukous and Amapiano from South Africa, spun by DJs like DJ KasBaby, DJ Ssese, Ashley and Kash Pro.

Then there's the city's very own miniature Las Vegas, Kabalagala strip, teeming with every nighttime watering hole imaginable, from sports bars, pubs and nightclubs to cocktail and pork joints. On Sundays, Kampalans brunch: head over to Drew & Jacs to cool down from the week's festivities, only to warm up (with shots) just in time for Monday, when the vicious cycle starts all over again.

Kampire

The breakout star of the burgeoning Ugandan dance scene, Kampire's played everywhere, from Diplo's Africa showcase at Sónar to Shanghai and Tokyo. A core member of the Nyege Nyege crew, her mixes pummel through the shadowy end of global bass, with a focus on diaspora sounds.

ANTI MASS

The radical queer collective (centred around the trio of Authentically Plastic, Nsasi and Turkana) started out pioneering safe parties in Kampala for their community before turning their hand to production with the *Doxa* EP during lockdown. They've also started running workshops for up-and-coming DJs to nurture the music scene that Nyege Nyege helped develop.

CLUBS

The Meat Guy

Named for the owner's humble beginnings as a meat vendor on the streets of Lugogo, this restaurant-cum-nightspot is located in a slender multi-storey building a little way off the beaten track in the dusty Industrial Area. Pay for your meat and liquor on entry and nab the best seats in the house with breathtaking views of the city skyline.

GUVNOR

Centrally located on Parliamentary Avenue, GUVNOR is one of Kampala's longest-running and most legendary nightclubs. Having gone through several phases of modernisation and expansion, as Kololo Night Club in the '60s to Ange-Noir in the '80s, the GUVNOR of today is one of the few spots that can offer a little something for everyone: special nights catering to expats, students, VIPs, and older generations brimming with nostalgia.

NYEGE NYEGE

Once a year, deep in the Ugandan forest along the banks of the River Nile, lies a pocket universe of electronic music. For four days, 300 artists from over 30 countries – ranging from traditional local dance troupes and rising East African selectors to international talent like Josey Rebelle, Shyboi and Juan Atkins – descend on Nyege Nyege Festival, delivering psychedelic percussion and hypnotic sets to the sweat-drenched crowds.

Ever since the near-catastrophic rainfall of its first instalment in 2015, the team behind Nyege Nyege have faced and overcome challenges on a scale many festivals couldn't imagine. "The first Nyege Nyege was a traumatic birth, to say the least," says co-founder and artistic director Derek Debru. "There were no sponsors, there wasn't even any security! We made a deal with the army that they would 'stand watch', so it was basically just a rave in the forest." Planned in just over a month in Uganda's wettest season, it rained like hell. Derek and co-founder Arlen gave out tickets and added to the 50+ line-up to make Nyege Nyege a hit... and it ate up their life savings. Since then, Derek's paid thousands to police and local power brokers that rock up yearly at Nyege Nyege's gates. "Everyone is out to hustle you, and the problem is, everybody thinks we're making a shitload of money!"

Darlyne (DJing as DECAY) has been a core member of Nyege Nyege collective since its inception. "The first Nyege Nyege was wild. It was a mad rush. Things like toilets? Security? Lights? Getting people to even come to the party? We didn't know what we were doing. It was just sweat and hope and the love for music. It poured. Everyone was slipping down the hills, tents were soaked. We had to cover the equipment with tarps, but even in that madness, people were so into it and kept dancing."

Things have progressed from that first event, when the team discovered there were only two CDJ decks in the whole country, but Darlyne still tells of stagehands running vinyl decks frantically between stages and the lengths reached to transport a Funktion-One system all the way from Kenya. Seven years on, Nyege Nyege is one of the most acclaimed festivals on the planet. A key destination for international bookers seeking a showcase of the amazing DJ and artist talent coming from the region, the crew have also taken on an ambassadorial role, nurturing the careers of artists like Menzi, Authentically Plastic and Rey Sapienz, with Darlyne and fellow crew member Kampire leading the charge.

DECAY (aka Darlyne), co-founder of Nyege Nyege, lights up the tropical disco stage

CAPE TOWN

Start your adventure at the record shop and finish up at the car wash (yeah)

Perched on the southern tip of the continent, surrounded by beaches and beautiful violet-capped mountains, Cape Town ('the Mother City') is one of the most picturesque cities on the planet, with a rich club culture that stretches back to the early jazz days and even before. The scene extends from small inner city clubs through to beach bars on the strips of Camps Bay, Kalk Bay or Hout Bay. There are also bigger beach clubs like Grand Africa and Cabo, introducing local and global audiences to a mix of sounds and acts (look out for Sunday afternoons in Cabo's '70s Laurel Canyon themed bar with DJs like the cosmic disco inclined El Gordo). There are parties at the many wine farms (Amelie Lens played an Ostrich Farm in 2022), and the outlying regions. Kayelitsha is home to Rands, an open air enclosure with a festival vibe where you can catch DJs like Saz playing hip-hop, live acts like Dee Koala, and deep house, amapiano and gqom. The loungey Kwa Ace is where you might find an emotional, spiritual take on house music from 'master of mixing' DJ Shimza.

There are frequent events in the suburbs and industrial areas like Paarden Eiland, and ultimately everything culminates in the centre of town, where the Mødular precinct has a truly credible underground feel, showcasing techno and house and constantly exploring new sounds with nights like VAULT and Killer Robot. Glitzier clubs like The Address and Chilli Bar push quality house, hip-hop and R'n'B. From amapiano and ggom, to house, hip-hop, traditional, jazz and techno, Cape Town boasts something for everyone. The real trick is getting a taste of it all. Be adventurous.

Online platforms like the CTEMF city guide are a great start, and fashion/nightlife platform SBCLTR on Instagram (@sb_cltr) are involved in a lot of what's good. But to really connect, start your odyssey at record stores like The Other Records or Roastin' (both in the Gardens neighbourhood), Mabu Vinyl (featured in the documentary *Searching For Sugarman*) or Voom Voom (a vintage spot in Observatory with a building that looks like something out of *Chitty Chitty Bang Bang*) to find out what's hot.

There's also a booming festival and outdoor culture in Cape Town. On most weekends, there are at least two to four open air options to choose from, including beach events like Bouzique. Bigger throwdowns include Cape Town Electronic Music Festival, Rocking The Daisies in October with the likes of Stormzy and Ari Lennox, and the 'techno-shamanic' Origin, where you'll find Kompakt Records's John Monkman alongside TOYTOY's Illing. Organik Love

○ RECORD SHOP

The Other Records Formerly jokingly referred to by its founders as "the smallest record store in Africa", Other grew out of a single table in a clothing store to become an essential stop for vinyl with in-store sessions, impromptu Sunday street parties and even a show on Gilles Peterson's Worldwide FM. A new location in the Gardens district has allowed the store to spread its wings.

Project, a three-day event at the lush Kromrivier Farm, hosts progressive local acts like ABRA, and the techy psytrance of Headroom. Indeed, it was the psytrance scene that pioneered festival culture here (with a healthy number of events from Vortex Parallel Universe to New Dawn and Madhaya still representing this), as well as exercising a strong influence on the aesthetic of almost every festival, where colourful psychedelic influences mesh with the local patterns and fabrics for the arenas and stages.

Back in the city though, perhaps the truest authentic Cape Town vibe is found on Sundays at the local *shisa nyama* (barbecue/meat roasts) and car washes scattered across the city's townships–some of the best music and parties in the country, and a cultural institution.

The entrance to Mødular, mixing underground, European-style clubbing with Cape Town's diversity

DJ / PRODUCER / LABEL

Leighton Moody
Anchor of the long-running We House Sundays parties at Paarden Eiland alongside fellow DJ Cassiem Latief, Moody has fused his love for jazz, soul and gospel into a unique take on deep house that has made him a fixture – and a crowd favourite – at every festival or event to hit Cape Town. His b2b Boiler Room Cape Town set with Cassiem is well worth digging out.

Rose Bonica
A visual artist, producer and live act who quit a boring tech job to embrace electronic music, the relentlessly creative Cape Town native Natalie-Rose Perel creates innovative yet danceable, darkly aggressive yet gentle adventures on the outer fringes of techno. Check out her Bandcamp, where the description of every release comes with a story behind its creation. A regular at Joburg's And Club and across her hometown, she made her overseas debut in 2019 at Berlin's Renate and released her debut album, the introspective *Tears for the Tea Maker* on her own label, Roses Are Red, in 2020.

NON
This highly conceptual label defines itself as a "collective of African artists, and of the diaspora, using sound as their primary media, to articulate the visible and invisible structures that create binaries in society, and in turn distribute power." In practical terms, that means showcasing adventurous electronica: Angel-Ho fusing noise and grime with Jersey club, or the muscular percussion and distorted synths of Nkisi.

CLUB / EVENT

Mødular
As you may have guessed from the flourish on the 'Ø', this downtown, 350-cap has a mission to mix underground, European style clubbing with the diversity of Cape Town. This includes a no photo rule, a community led culture, LGBTQ+ inclusion, and a music policy built around residents like Deano, and the prolific Ivan Turanjanin, who fuses Detroit-influenced techno with a wide range of influences to create stunning soundscapes. Guests have included Ryan Elliott and Anthony Parasole, while new upstairs space Lido has house music, breakbeat and other eclectic club sounds.

Cape Town Electronic Music Festival (CTEMF)
Bringing names like Ame, Job Jobse and Deetron to Cape Town to play alongside SA stars like Da Capo, the city's biggest electronic event, held in the vast Atlantic Studios in Milnerton, pivoted in lockdown to stream SA artists and throw a festival on Bandcamp.

JOH ANN ESB URG

From amapiano and Afro House parties in Soweto to underground techno at TOYTOY, Thursday can't some soon enough

Joburg is a hard-working city, the engine of South Africa's economic renewal, and the club scene here only happens from Thursday to Sunday. But when it goes, it goes *off*. A typical weekend might begin somewhere like Parkhurst (a student area with bars like Jolly Cool) or Maboneng (a vibey neighbourhood with lots of restaurants and bars like Living Room, CURIOCITY and Arts On Main). Or perhaps on the Melville strip, in the bars of 7th Street – maybe Hell's Kitchen (an American style whiskey bar) or the grungy Smoking Kills.

Later, you might head 10 minutes south in a cab to Braamfontein, home of Kitchener's Carvery, the second-oldest bar in Johannesburg. Complete with original 1906 fixtures and fittings, it somehow transforms into a dancefloor on Friday, with nights like Coquette Sessions (with DJs like DJ Okapi exploring South Africa's forgotten pop gems) and Unleash the Wolf (showcasing South African electronic artists like !Sooks) untill 3.30am. You'll also find new spot The Playground in Braamfontein, a market with live music, and it's a short walk across the Nelson Mandela Bridge to Newtown and the leading underground venue And Club, home for 10 years to techno institution TOYTOY. Newtown was one of Johannesburg's largest industrial hubs until the 1980s, when it was abandoned by industry, leaving empty warehouses and derelict grain silos. These structures stood vacant until the early '90s when promoters in South Africa's burgeoning rave scene began to throw raves in them, aptly named 'the silos' – And Club, which moved there in 2015, is the spiritual successor to that scene.

Just around the corner, Carfax, a corrugated iron former industrial space, hosts nights ranging from techno and psytrance to drum'n'bass and deep house, alongside art exhibitions and live music. You'll also glimpse the Ponte apartment block on the horizon, a striking piece of Brutalist architecture that fell into disrepair and disrepute soon after being built (with rubbish piled up as high as the 14th floor of the central courtyard), before being rejuvenated in the late 2010s into the most prestigious address in the admittedly still slightly dodgy Hillbrow district.

South Africa's home-grown talent, Black Coffee

You might also choose to begin your night in Soweto. Once another symbol of poverty, oppression and the struggle against apartheid, the former township is now one of Joburg's most vibrant areas. Here you'll find bar/restaurants like Cafe Hangova and Kofifi, and clubs like the vast Zone 6 (a 4,000-cap mega club complete with two arenas and even a swimming pool) and the recently opened KONKA, a hotspot for hip-hop and amapiano (look out for the likes of Kabza de Small).

To a European audience used to compartmentalising everything into distinct genres, electronic music from South Africa breaks down into the electronic rap groove of kwaito, the loose groove of gqom, the slowed-down garage style of midtempo and the soulful, Pretoria-originated adaptation of piano-led house music, amapiano. Yet in practice, DJs in places like Zone 6 or Kong club in Rosebank are just as likely to mix genres under the broad banner of 'house music' (or Afro House, as it's often broadly referred to in Europe), in the same way that Black and white South Africans mix and meet on the dancefloor. As Black Coffee says, "house music found a home here because it has a certain

The amazing psychadelic visuals of Twilight festival

○ RECORD SHOP

Mr Vinyl
This sleek store, located in the stylishly repurposed 1930s industrial precinct of 44 Stanley, is recognisable by the stylised image of a spinning record on the large main window and home to one of the city's largest collections of new and used vinyl, a selection of turntables, plus a couch and coffee table for weary seekers.

DJ Buhle

Soweto born and bred, DJ Buhle has been a cornerstone of the South African house scene since the mid 2000s as part of the BFR DJ crew in the township's Orlando West, a hothouse for a generation of pioneering South African DJs like Claude and Mbuso. She launched the *Mixmag* Lab Johannesburg in 2019 alongside Seth Troxler and De Capo.

Themba

Raved about as SA's next big thing when he released on Hot Since 82's Knee Deep In Sound and on Yoshitoshi in 2018, Themba was already two decades into a career as one of the country's leading DJs. Spinning at some of Johannesburg's biggest clubs during his university days at the turn of the century, it was under the name Euphonik that he became known for his radio mixes and scored a job as A&R at South Africa's seminal dance label Soul Candi, putting together tracks for their compilations. As Themba, he's now in demand across the world.

Super Black Tapes

Founded by Joburg's Fred Buddah and Ofuren in 2011 as Roots Go Deep Music before a rebranding in 2015, Super Black Tapes releases music solely from African artists and has been the launchpad for a generation of deep house and techno producers ever since, including the founders and Brother Aten, CodeKid and Migzor.

Techno institution TOYTOY, housed in the famous And Club

CLUB / EVENT

And Club

The standard-bearer for Johannesburg's underground scene, And Club is a minimal and concrete dance space with moody lighting, a gritty atmosphere and a strict no phone, no camera policy (with an attached garden open in the warmer months). Friday nights belong to flagship TOYTOY, dedicated to techno with residents like Dogstarr, Illing and Fabio and guests from DVS1 to Charlotte de Witte, while Saturdays rotate between Jullian Gomes (deep house), Teknotribe (psytrance and hard techno) and Science Frikshun (drum'n'bass with Sol Pillars and RudeOne). Look out for the club kids pushing their own eccentric fashion style.

Twilight / It's Personal Picnic

Johannesburg's rainy season is summer time, which isn't conducive to outdoor festivals, but Twilight Open Air in November has brought the likes of Rustie to the city, and the It's Personal Picnic, held in the James & Ethel Gray Park, is a perfect fit for the dreamy techno of acts like Stimming.

DJ Buhle performs outside

LAGOS

From the mainland to the island (though possibly not back again) Lagos is a clubbing – and music – superpower

The centre of Africa's music industry, and one of the most hard-partying cities on the continent, Lagos's music scene is split between 'the Island' – home of wealthy pop stars and the biggest clubs – and the mainland, where aspiring musicians and producers launch new styles and tracks, hoping that a few weeks later they'll have taken the island by storm.

On the island, the best place to begin is SOUTHsouth. The Friday night social in this restaurant-cum-DJ bar is where younger clubbers meet to swap plans for the weekend, gossip and mix around 10pm or 11pm, before either heading out to the clubs at about 2am or 3am or heading back to the mainland. DJ Honeay holds court every Friday, spinning the city's typical open format mix of primarily Nigerian pop music (artists like Wizkid, Davido, the British-born Central Cee, to name a few) and occasionally a little South African ampiano or US house and hip-hop. DJs who specialise in one genre or refuse to play the hits don't tend to go down well in Lagos: 90 per cent are 'open format', albeit with a heavy focus on Nigerian pop music or styles like street hop that have penetrated the mainstream.

Clubs on the island include the huge Zorya, a massive, full-on Miami style bottle service and glam club that nevertheless holds its own musically, and Bolivar. The latter is the current home of local legend DJ Obi, a Lagos DJ whose crowd will follow him around the city wherever he plays. Nights on the island for the bed-shy tend to finish up at places like strip club Silver Fox,prized more as an afterhours hangout than for its pole dancing(strip club culture has never really taken off here), and intense pop star and industry hangout DNA, which is often still packed at 5am.

The mainland has its own giant venues, like the humongous Cubana, but here the scene is built even more around parties than buildings. Nights and promotions are extremely nomadic, often moving week to week. Look out for Element House, a party at the centre of the house music scene; Village Sound System, helmed by former nurse Sensei Lo who mixes Afropop, electronic, R'n'B and alté, topped up with the special "Sensei Lo Hot Sauce" – highlighting percussive notes in the mix; or Bang Bang Tuesday, run by a female duo whose return to the city after an absence was hugely welcomed by midweek clubbers. The mainland is where Nigeria's hugely fertile music culture blooms at events like Mainland Block Party. Lagos's clubbers tend to go out in large groups of 10 or even 15, taking the party with them as they move around by car or taxi, and are wary of travelling between the mainland and island after midnight, when hassle from the police on the street can become common.

DJ Obi performs at a Mixmag party in Lagos

DJS / LABEL

DJ Obi
A former holder of the world record for the longest ever DJ set (240 hours... he says he suffered hallucinations along the way), Obi's intensely loyal following rejoiced when he found a regular home at Obi's House on a Monday night at Bolivar. Playing a mixture of Nigerian pop and open format in his hometown, he's toured everywhere from London to Ibiza.

Mavin Records
After running more than 10 years, Don Jazzy's Mavin Records is among the top-tier of global imprints, a star-making machine that puts out artists from across the African continent in styles such as Afropop and Afrobeats. Hits include Rema's 'Soundgasm' and 'Bounce', and Ladipoe's 'Feeling', and Mavin also regularly breaks new names such as young artists Ayra Starr and Magixx.

CLUBS / EVENT

Fela Kuti / New Afrika shrine
No music lover's trip to Lagos is complete without a pilgrimage to the former home of the nation's favourite son until his death in 1997. Now a 2,500-cap venue, you can watch his descendants Femi, Seun and Made rehearse all week before they take charge of their respective nights across the weekend– often alongside international guests including Skepta and Lauryn Hill. Entry is often free.

Mainland Block Party
Growing out of an event in the garden of a burger bar in the Ikeja neighbourhood in 2018 to become Nigeria's biggest party, MBP now hosts thousands every month at a variety of locations across the city, while incubating some of Lagos' freshest new sounds and artists like Ladipoe and Alpha P.

○ RECORD SHOP

Jazzhole
Home to one of the most astonishing collections of second-hand records on the planet. Jazzhole owner Kunle Tejuosho has been building the collections since the '80s, and is justifiably protective of it – there is even a section of records he considers too precious to sell, and others he won't let leave the country. The space hosts art shows, and the café serves 40 varieties of tea.

TEL AVIV

This hectic, dense city always seems perched on the edge of political crisis – no wonder it's so committed to hedonism

"There's a well known saying, 'dance like there's no tomorrow'," says Tel Aviv DJ Deep'a. "Living in this part of the world, you sometimes really don't know what will happen tomorrow, and this feeling translates to a very instant vibe in our nightlife."

Tel Aviv has a reputation as a city committed to hedonism, and the centre of that commitment is the Teder, a permanently packed open plaza ringed with galleries and arcades holding clubs, bars and restaurants. Tune in online to Teder.FM ahead of time to acclimatise. One of those clubs is Rafi, where Ohad Peleg's Sadan Records parties, built around their electro meets hip-hop meets UKG-inflected sound, are starting to offer an alternative to the dominance of techno. But if techno is what you're after, beyond the Teder, the Berlin vault-style Breakfast Club and The Block (famed for its astonishing sound system), have everything you need – The Block in particular is a favourite with international visitors like Ben Klock and Michael Mayer. Look out also for back-alley bar Sputnik. Florentin is one of the most buzzing areas, packed with bars, but also with some handily undeveloped industrial space such as warehouse Haoman 17, sometime home of gay facing techno night Pag, famed for transforming venues with lights, projections and performers.

Clubbers don't drink very much in Tel Aviv, perhaps because of the prices: one double gin and tonic in a club is the equivalent of over £15/$20. Indeed, runaway rents and the high cost of living mean a lot of young people live pay cheque to pay cheque, working two jobs with no savings – combined with the constant political tension, this may explain the mass catharsis of nights out in the city.

There are of course thorny ethical questions to clubbing here, and for artists playing the country. Tel Aviv's club and art scene is one of the few generally safe spaces for Palestinian artists and clubbers to engage culturally, but some Palestinian (and indeed international) artists refuse to play the city as part of the cultural boycott of Israel, considering its liberal image of beaches and parties as a fig leaf for the occupation. Yup, thorny. Sincere curiosity about the political issues is unlikely to be met by the locals with hostility, but it's worth sussing out the company you're in first. Tel Aviv's incorporated Palestinian 'twin town' of Jaffa, is where Arabs Do It Better (the name is tongue in cheek, the party is run by an Israeli and a Palestinian, David Pearl and Marwan Hawash) host their parties celebrating a confluence of electronic and Arabic music they call "electronic hafla".

Shabbas (the Jewish Sabbath) means no public transport from sundown on Fridays until sundown on Saturdays: Thursday is Tel Aviv's Friday night. Outside the city, the UV-painted spectre of psytrance looms heavy in the desert parties and raves, but look out for Parallele's industrial techno events, run by a collective of visual artists, which are constantly shifting location to stay one step ahead of the authorities. Tel Aviv's clubbers like their music hard and intense – no time for subtle warm-ups here – and have adopted a couple of Arab phrases as their watchword: you'll hear "Yalla!" ("come on/let's go!") and "Sababa" ("everything is great") a lot, at least if things are going well.

DJS / LABEL

Tom Koren
A key player in the continuing evolution of Tel Aviv's scene, with a style that ranges wildly across genres from R'n'B to baile funkvia house and ambient. Look out for her team-ups with hip-hop artist Kidnappa Koko and parties with her all-woman DJ crew, Salty.

Deep'a & Biri
Israeli duo Deep'a & Biri became involved in the Tel Aviv club scene after completing their three years of compulsory national service (Biri absconded one weekend to play a DJ set and wound up in jail for 30 days). Their second album, *Dominance* (released on their own Black Crow label in 2018) was inspired by an especially long, cold winter in their part-time home Berlin, and the resulting sound is dark and cerebral, characterised by fusing ethereal ambient sounds with harder pulses.

Fortuna Records
On a mission to re-issue lost music from the region, from Israeli psychedelia to Middle Eastern grooves, Fortuna are also a DJ crew who put on regular showcases at the Teder, while members like DJ Hectik and Turtle have played clubs across Europe.

CLUBS

Phi
A free, open air summer venue with a stunning terrace, decks in a cage and a strong LGBTQ+ vibe thanks to parties like Queer Cast, Phi is a key venue behind the burgeoning leftfield breaks scene, and a platform for emerging artists like Uzi and DJ Catfish.

The Block
Gilles Peterson describes the Block as "the perfect balance between industrial and cosy", but ultimately this club, now on its second location, is a decade-and-a-half exercise by founder and DJ Yaron Trax in constructing the perfect club sound system. The result is a sonic wonder of the world.

○ RECORD SHOP

Nuweiba
Located inside the Teder complex, this shop, listening room and bar/hangout hosts all kinds of off-beat events among the vinyl, from Hebrew hip-hop live performances to radio broadcasts.

195

Performers at Pag's performance at Grounded Festival

A Pag party at Haoman 17 with Deep'a and Biri behind the decks

Chapter 5

ASIA & OCEANIA

Seoul

Bali

Seoul

Bali

Taipei

Krung Th
Taipei
Seoul
Tōkyō
Bali
Sydney
Goa
Melbourne

Sydney
Melbourne
Krung Thep
...dū
Goa
Tōkyō

GOA

India's club capital has been a party and alternative lifestyle destination since the global hippie counterculture flocked here in the '60s and '70s

IZiKi Goa party at Prana Anjuna, home to some of the most interesting music in the region

Hippies flocked to Goa in the '60s and '70s, drawn by paradisiacal surroundings, liberal laws on hashish and endorsement by the likes of the Beatles. The heyday of the Goa trance sound, which developed out of this hippie culture to spread worldwide, was the early '90s. But while the era of the anything-goes five-day trance parties may be over, Goa is still the epicentre of electronic music in the world's most populous country, and the unique vibe still persists: a little bit Ibiza, a little mad hippie energy and, of course, the hackneyed-but-true quirks that characterise this country – yep, including cows wandering around dancefloors.

India's new middle class, and much of its music industry, have embraced Goa over the past few years. Beyond its stunning beaches and landscape, it has a club scene and culture that, compared to much of the rest of the country (and perhaps due to its European legacy as a Portuguese colony until the '70s), is perceived as more liberal, cosmopolitan and less regimented. The shift towards local tourism accelerated during the pandemic, as foreign tourism – both incoming and outgoing – became more difficult. Meanwhile, the traditional gender imbalance of Indian nightlife has changed dramatically in the last few years as more middle class women and girls have asserted their independence, to the vast benefit of the scene.

The new visitors prefer their music fast and hard, and while the trademark trance that built the scene persists, the global techno juggernaut has become the dominant sound, with artists like German techno producer Modeplex, Brazil's Wehbba and Mumbai's Bullzeye packing the floors. But there is a growing and exciting house and Afro House scene in some of the smaller venues and parties. And there are a lot of venues here. Most are concentrated in the north of the province, around the towns of Anjuna and Morjim.

In Anjuna, HillTop is one venue with a long trance heritage that, besides events hosted by psytrance labels like Parvati Records, has started to pivot towards heavier techno acts such as Nina Kraviz. Curlies on Vagator Beach may be a throwback to the hippie days, but the nearby Pinakin hosts some of the best local talent, and the historic 9Bar, open since 1976, has recently been revamped with the addition of the Mirage Beach Club and weekly techno. Salud, a breathtaking clifftop venue overlooking Ozran Beach, hosts the *Mixmag* Lab Goa.

Morjim hosts the massive Ibiza-style Marbela and the Living Room, as well as a revolving cast of big commercial clubs and smaller boutique pop-ups, while Shahpura's strip, so long the main hippie drag, is now a hangout for Bollywood stars as much as acid casualties. And then there are the festivals: the famous Sunburn, Krank (focused on local DJs like Calm Chor and Shaun Moses) and Satellite (house and techno on a beach with acts like Funkagenda) are among the biggest, but countless outdoor parties take place either side of monsoon season. Besides the big festivals, partying all night and sleeping through the often punishingly hot days is normal here.

Sunburn, the biggest EDM festival in India

DJS / PRODUCERS / LABEL

Anyasa
The first Indian artist ever to release on Above & Beyond's iconic Anjuna labels (after 21 years), Anish Sood, aka Anyasa, found success early in his career, riding the Indian dance music explosion, headlining mega festivals like Sunburn and supporting touring artists from Black Coffee to Dixon. But a lockdown focus on working with Indian vocalists and instrumentalists, fusing classical Indian music with influences from Chicago house to Goa trance, led to his 2021 masterwork, the *Gaya* EP.

Shaun Moses
A key figure behind the rise of techno in India, Goan native Moses is a stalwart of the club and festival scene in the province, and one of a handful of Indian DJs who perform across the globe. His releases on Senso Sounds, Tronic, Octopus and Secret Cinema's Gem label are a dark, weighty take on the genre.

Discokid
A particular favourite at the *Mixmag* Lab Goa parties at Salut, Fatema Hakim, aka DJ Discokid, doesn't just play joyous, synth-inflected modern disco music, she also hosts one of the most stylish boutique parties in the area: Paradise Disco at the Ibiza-style C'est La Vie beach bar in Badem.

Soupherb
Founded by pioneering Indian DJs Ash Roy and Calm Chor, Soupherb has an eclectic range but specialises in the sweet spot between acidic, grooving and minimal techno, and features artists from across the globe, from Chile's Matías Sapag to Mumbai's Decode Blue.

CLUB / EVENT

Prana Anjuna
This tiny Anjuna beach shack venue is home to some of the most interesting music in the region, at the centre of the nascent house and Afro House scene. Look out for the Jungle Stories and Afronight events with guests like Zokhuma and Merak. The incredible sunsets, food, and cocktails help, too.

Sunburn
Recently returned to its birthplace of Goa after a few years of exile in Pune, this huge December festival is the closest thing to Tomorrowland in this part of the world: three days of huge international EDM acts like Martin Garrix, Chainsmokers and DJ Snake interspersed with the likes of Maceo Plex and Luciano, lavish production, pyrotechnics and aspirational, Instagrammable spectacle.

Drag queen Mystic Curl performs at Prana Anjuna's Queerious Ball in 2021

203

GOA TRANCE

"Since the '60s when the first hippies landed here from San Francisco, Goa has always been on the legendary hippie trail," says producer Anyasa. And Goa trance is very much rooted in that lineage. It was born from a fusion of the later hippie sound – noodling psychedelic rock with increasingly electronic influences – and the post punk experimental electronica coming from Europe in the '80s: particularly the EBM or 'electronic body music' of bands like Nitzer Ebb, Front 242 and Front Line Assembly. This new style of music – with its sequenced repetitive basslines, programmed rhythms and shouted lyrics – encouraged ecstatic dancing and had enough weirdness to satisfy the bohemian palate, growing in demand from DJs on the Goan scene like Fred Disko, Dr Bobby and Goa Gil. EBM was a precursor of the trance and techno genres across the world, but it was the local influence that made the Goa trance sound unique.

With a history reaching back over 6,000 years, Indian classical is one of the oldest formal music systems and one of the richest in existence, often characterised by multiple instrumentation, driving hypnotic rhythms and repetitive vocals that can bring on a trance-like state in the listener. Combine that influence with the proliferation of mind-altering substances and marathon outdoor parties in search of a soundtrack, and a new genre was born. As the KLF, Sven Väth and Jam & Spoon were defining the early trance sound in Europe, Goa, by now a destination for DJs of all styles from all over the world, started to develop its own take: organic and spiritual, characterised by atmospheric intros, layers of Eastern influenced melodies, sci-fi samples and lengthy run times extended by special edits. The DJs who played in Goa would often mix from DATs (high quality Digital Audio Tapes a little smaller than the standard audio cassette favoured by jam band enthusiasts recording live bootlegs in the US), not just for the hippie connection but because vinyl could often warp and melt in the strong Goa heat.

The first release that collected the sound for a global audience was *Project II Trance*, released in 1993 by Dragonfly Records and featuring artists like Gumbo, Genetic, The Infinity Project, Total Eclipse and Mandra Gora, while Paul Oakenfold's 1994 two-hour *The Goa Mix* truly put the genre on the map. By the mid '90s, there were parties championing the sound springing up across the globe, including the huge Megatripolis in the UK and GAIA festival in France, as well as a healthy scene in Australia.

Goa trance's time in the sunlight would be limited; by the millenium it had been superseded even in Goa by the more minimal and visceral psytrance sound, perhaps better suited to the proliferation of stimulants overtaking psychedelics as the party drugs of choice. But it's still a source of inspiration for artists exploring the fusion of electronic music with local influences.

Anjuna Beach in the 1970s

TOKYO

Japan's fragile scene blossoms in Shibuya, where underground venues champion new talent alongside international names

Still reeling from the closure of multi-roomed mega club ageHa in 2022, several of the biggest clubs in Tokyo have suffered from tying their destiny to big name EDM, neglecting the nurture of electronic subcultures in favour of table service, wall-to-wall LED screens, and celebrity DJ imports and their escalating fees. And that's important. Club culture in Japan is still to an extent a niche, sometimes even frowned upon, in a country where an ageing, conservative generation holds the reins culturally, economically and politically. Japanese clubbers – musically knowledgeable, passionate and open-minded – often tend to be private about their enthusiasms in their weekday lives. Building and nurturing the scene here takes work and it remains, to an extent, a fragile thing; dancing in clubs after midnight was technically illegal here until 2015, electronic music rarely troubles the charts, and club culture has never really penetrated the mainstream.

That said, there is a vibrant club scene in Tokyo, and it is centred on the 15km square ward of Shibuya. Famous for its fashion district of Harajuku – where the pictures of folk dressed as anime schoolgirls or '50s bikers come from – Shibuya is the home of much of Tokyo's nightlife and youth culture, and was the first ward in the country to recognise same sex partnerships. It's where you'll find clubs from the intimate and resolutely underground VENT (close to Harajuku, and where Andrew Weatherall played his last Japanese gig in 2019) to the massive (by Tokyo standards) WOMB. Both champion upcoming and established Japanese talent from Alice Iguchi to Takaaki Itoh and Nobu alongside international acts.

Festivals here – from Ultra Japan and Electric Daisy Carnival through to the techno-focused Labyrinth– tend to be family affairs with a psychedelic-yet-harmonious vibe. In the clubs, drugs are rare, alcohol isn't consumed in great quantities, and the atmosphere on dancefloors is correspondingly a little less than intense, despite the universality of incredible sound systems. Solo clubbing is common, with pre-club drinking in groups less so. One ritual that is important to the Tokyo scene, though, is the post-club meal – Ramen, deep fried chicken, Japanese curry – fuel for what can often be a long journey back home on the dawn train.

Tokyo lit up by night

Keep an eye on *Mixmag Japan*'s website for the latest club news and events, but perhaps the best way to experience club culture in Tokyo is to come out of the Shibuya, Shinjuku or Shimokitazawa stations and walk the streets with a Japanese beer in your hand. Make friends, ask the people working the door what's happening inside, and people-watch. Just remember, peering through the windows won't do you any good: in this vertical city, clubs are rarely found on the ground floor.

Dancers are engulfed in WOMB's immersive lightshow

Ken Ishii DJs at Contact & Vision

DJS

Ken Ishii
The key figure in Japan's techno scene for decades, Ishii debuted on R&S Records way back in 1993 and has consistently showcased his unique take on Detroit techno on labels like !K7 and Harthouse, among many others, ever since. A popular, approachable figure, he's an icon for Japanese artists and as a DJ frequently plays across Tokyo when he's not touring the world.

Powder
The buzz around Nagasaki-born Powder started in 2015 with her debut Spray on Stockholm-based imprint Born Free, and three more followed in the coming years, running through anything from ambient sounds to intense industrial psych-disco. In 2019, she was tapped by Tim Sweeney's Beats In Space Records to put together the inaugural mix in an offshoot series for an episode called *Powder in Space*. The mix was an instant classic, an off-kilter journey spanning glitch, ambient, psychedelia, acid house, classical and more.

DJ Nobu
A DJ with roots in punk and hardcore, Nobu had been playing in Japan since the '90s before an epochal appearance at Berghain in 2010 put him on the wishlist of every boutique festival, forward-thinking booker and aficionado on the planet. With a mystique comparable to the likes of DJ Harvey, Nobu's cerebral, psychedelic post punk take on house and techno was perfected at his legendary Future Terror parties, which began in his hometown of Chiba and passed the 20th anniversary mark in 2021.

CLUBS

VENT
This basement venue opened in 2016 in Minato and is famed for its cutting edge sound design, with architecture that focuses the music on the crowd with the same precision as the raking beams of light that sweep the dancefloor. Two areas are separated by a concrete wall with a line-up that focuses on established Japanese talent, like the fantastic techno adventurer Mars89, Powder and Frankie $ alongside up-and-comers, while Maya Jane Coles, Midland and Red Axes have all passed through.

WOMB
The most famous club in Tokyo with a capacity of 1,000, WOMB is soundtracked by an array of dance music styles from drum'n'bass to techno. The diverse line-ups mix underground artists with the more mainstream: Richie Hawtin, Marco Carola, Joseph Capriati and Friction have all graced the hi-tech DJ booth, while the club also fosters local talent throughout the week. Expect peerless sound and an incredible, immersive light show.

Dancers at WOMB

O RECORD SHOP

Technique
While Technique's newest physical location in Shibuya sadly didn't last long (the shop is now online only), it's still Tokyo's best source for electronic music, with the newest house and techno releases from both local and international record labels and a deep used section for those looking for a (virtually) dusty session searching for rare finds.

LISTENING BARS

Listening bar culture in Japan has to be understood in the context of the post WWII occupation of the country by the US. GIs brought with them many things that were embraced by a country looking abroad for new influences and experiences, from whisky to baseball to jazz. More specifically, jazz records. In an age when international tours were rare, the Japanese took jazz to their hearts, and vinyl was expensive enough that enthusiasts would often have to gather together to share the listening experience.

Meanwhile, a moral panic about the sanctity of Japanese female virtue in the face of the vast numbers of GIs led first to the creation of huge official brothels and later a crackdown on 'dance halls', which were viewed not only as a worrying American cultural influence but also places where prostitution was common. In 1948, the Fueiho law was introduced, stipulating that only clubs with a floor space larger than 710sq ft could allow dancing, and a later amendment resulted in a ban on all dancing after midnight. Combining these two factors with a long-standing culture of tiny, single owner, idiosyncratic side street bars and cafés in Japan's cities led to the first listening bars in the '50s. These were often built around the jazz passions of their owner, where silence was encouraged and the space often shaped to emphasise the acoustics. Going to a café and listening to a new release as a group became the norm for a generation of Japanese jazz fans. At its height, areas like Tokyo's Shibuya and Shinjuku had dozens of *jazz kissa*, as the cafes are known locally, scattered around them.

The third factor was also linked to Japan's postwar evolution: the design and production of high-quality electronics. While Japan's club scene may be small in comparison to other countries, its technological impact on club and DJ culture is unrivalled. Japan's Pioneer is responsible for the modern DJ booth, inventing the CDJ and the DJ mixer as we know it. Osaka's Roland corporation, with its TR-909 and TR-808 drum machines and its work developing MIDI, played a bigger role in the development of modern music than any company in history. The country has led the way in developing high fidelity audio for decades, as well as nurturing an appreciation of quality sound as a key part of club culture. Building on the legacy of the jazz bars, owners passionate about electronic music – and let's be honest, those who also enjoyed nerding out on sound quality and equipment – started to open their own listening bars in Japan's cities in the '90s (the renowned SHeLTeR, opened in 1989, was one of the first), even inviting DJs to curate the playlist. Within a few years, overseas tourists and Japanophiles would discover them, often causing tension when a careless recommendation in the press would lead to hordes of noisy hipsters descending on a bar and shattering the tranquillity. On the plus side, listening bar culture and aesthetic has now spread around the globe, with music lovers from London's Spiritland and Brilliant Corners to New York's Eavesdrop able to find sonic sanctuaries.

JBS, a vinyl listening bar in Tokyo

BANGKOK

The Hangover may have to look elsewhere for a sequel, but the afterparty never ended in Bangkok, no matter what those 'men in brown' say

Bangkok today is not the raucous party capital it once was. The lawless anarchy that once attracted bachelor parties en masse to anything-goes clubs where decadence and debauchery were served on a silver platter with a side of Eurodance doesn't exist any more – largely due to an accelerated police presence in the city, which locals would say only became a bother around the time of the 2014 coup d'état. While the parties live on, it's been a bit different ever since.

Just before the coup, clubs like GLOW, Bed Supperclub and 808 RCA thrived, bringing in heavyweight international DJs weekly, and educating club goers in experiencing something other than the mainstream. These clubs paved the way for the development of an electronic scene, but the next generation of parties in Bangkok would involve more intimate venues, smaller clubs and a more refined taste in music. Bed Supperclub closed in 2013 after nearly 11 years of operations, and today Sing Sing Theater is its second coming, with thanks to founder Sanya Souvanna Phouma. The club belongs to a family of aesthetically unique venues designed by Ashley Sutton and, despite its models and bottles association, it still manages to garner the respect of the underground for booking DJs like Sébastien Léger, YokoO, Red Axes, Pan-Pot and Amine K.

Competition comes from smaller spaces like 12 x 12, Tropic City, De Commune, Studio Lam and Mustache, the latter being a late-night haunt that, for several years, was the city's de facto afterparty jam, famed for its out-of-centre location and persistently broken air conditioning. Mustache in its original location has now closed and operates out of VHS on Friday and Saturday nights. These smaller venues have become something of a safe haven far away from police raids, making them a favourite among club goers looking to avoid the big city hassle of traffic and the notorious men in brown – known for stopping taxis carrying foreigners and drug testing them on the spot.

The rising popularity of intimate, off-the-beaten-track venues has given local crews the opportunity to develop identities and build fan bases. Many of them have gone on to start brands and labels like Kolour, Karma Klique, UNST, Kandoo, Mustache, Grow Room and Disco Diaries. These promoters lean more on interesting locations than fixed clubs and are really the driving force of current-day music culture in Bangkok. But with a curfew of somewhere between midnight and 2am for much of the last decade, it's been a rough run for all nightlife in Bangkok. The afterparties never died, though – at the time of writing, they're bubbling at Never Normal in Lat Phrao.

DJS

Sunju Hargun
One of Thailand's biggest international exports, Sunju has become a household name across the region for playing spaced-out music in forests, warehouses and castles in Thailand. If you're wondering why you haven't heard of him, maybe you've been listening to his Mogambo and Khun Fluff aliases, which manifest on periodic ambient albums released on one of the many locally spun labels he's associated with.

Mendy Indigo
Starting her career in her hometown of Korat on a borrowed computer before moving onto the infamous island parties of southern Thailand where she really cut her teeth, Mendy Indigo's transition to big city and big club was an easy one with her dark and melodic take on techno. Mendy's rags-to-rave story has caught the attention of media and music fans all over the world and even landed her a feature spot in *Mixmag*'s 2018 Global Dancefloor series alongside Nakadia. She was also the first-ever female Thai DJ to play Ibiza's Circoloco.

Siamese Twins
A home for authentic, tribally rooted sounds by Asian artists, the label creates symbiotic dialogues with producers around the globe. Dually run by artists in Thailand and Taiwan, its releases lean towards more slow-burning soundscapes, like heady ambient with tinges of Goa trance that weave in the Thai and Khmer concept of sacred mantras.

More Rice
This Bangkok-based record label-cum-record store focuses on releasing artists from Asia with a distinctly regional touch thanks to its rice-inspired aesthetic –an extra tasty treat for those who order releases on vinyl. Alongside a couple of best-of-Asia compilations, the label has released music from Sarayu, Doildoshi, Tarsius and DOTT.

The Solar Stage at Wonderfruit, an otherworldly four-day celebration of music, art, food and ideas

CLUB / EVENT

BEAM
BEAM opened in 2016, with Dave Parry helming the launch, and features a body kinetic dancefloor alongside one of the city's first VOID Acoustics sound systems. Offering a warehouse-style experience, the club launched with lofty aspirations and sought bookings like Tom Trago, M.A.N.D.Y., Eli & Fur, TOKiMONSTA, Soul Clap, Carl Craig and Marcel Dettmann before pivoting towards a more local Thai-style approach, namely hip-hop and commercial house. They still occasionally pull some big electronic names.

Wonderfruit
Oft lauded by the media as the 'Burning Man of the East', Wonderfruit is an other-wordly four-day celebration of art, music, food and ideas all presented with a whimsical Thai twist and sustainability at its core. Taking place annually in Pattaya, the festival has hosted artists like Acid Pauli, Richie Hawtin, Floating Points, Craig Richards, Four Tet and many more over six years, with a line-up that is always well-balanced with local acts; look out for a stage called the Molam Bus, where you'll hear rural folk music from around the region.

BEIJING

Homegrown club crews and artists have replaced imported stars in the historic Chinese capital – and it's all the better for it

Inside Zhao Dai, the petri dish of Chinese club culture

Early voyagers into China's clubbing scene would have found a Eurocentric and expat-driven set of clubs in Beijing, but recent years have seen a significant shift in the underground ethos of the city. Undoubtedly restricted at times by the stranglehold of China's party politics, felt more tangibly in Beijing than any other of the Eastern cities (this was, after all, the scene of the Tiananmen Square massacre of so many free-thinking young people in 1989 – no Second Summer Of Love here), the capital has still provided ample space for some of China's most radical art and the communities behind it.

From afar, a skyline dominated by tower blocks suggests a smoggy symbol of modern capitalist society, but few cities of such scale retain a sense of history in the way that Beijing does. Packed with ancient parks and palaces, and with a distinctly more 'traditional' Chinese atmosphere than the equally developed Shanghai, Beijing is a picture of 21st-century China in its own image. Beijing's rapid development has created a perceived identity crisis, but flip this around, and you'll find a cultural congruence that is pushing the Beijing art scene into unchartered and exciting territory. It is here that musicians like Howie Lee, Meng Qi and Jason Hou have excavated cultural motifs like traditional Chinese instruments and field-recorded sounds, merging them with futuristic sound design. Just as China's famous dancing aunties can be spotted twirling in tandem across the city's parks and plazas, pockets of countercultural dancers unite in techno clubs and punk bars, defiant of the monotonal soundtracks of many of the city's more commercial nightlife areas.

In the Eastern district of Chaoyang, one of the city's most happening areas, crowds skip between Zhao Dai and the 200-cap Wigwam, with many of the same faces popping up at the two nearby-ish venues, often on the same night. Both staunchly loyal to local DJs, the two clubs feel like siblings despite their different owners, and together form the new centre of electronic music in Beijing, a city which had previously looked largely to Western artists for its moments of clubbing inspiration. Older fixtures in the scene like Dada and Lantern still hold their own in that part of town, offering a mix of home-grown and imported selectors, from Pei's regular ByBeyDisco parties at Dada to Portuguese-Macau artist Ngls playing across the different clubs. Arguably in its healthiest state since Western dance music first reached China, the Beijing underground offers plenty of its own creations to explore, and numerous venues to explore it in.

Howie Lee
It's almost impossible to overstate the influence that Howie Lee has had on China's fledgling electronic music scene. Arguably the face of Do Hits, the idiosyncratic producer led the charge away from European and American techno and trap tones towards an altogether new sound, and one genuinely deserving of the overused tag of 'innovation'. Forging an unlikely partnership between traditional Chinese sounds and Western bass music, Lee's early work moved between trap rhythms and ambient gameboy-esque soundscapes, evolving over the years to defy notions of genre altogether.

Slowcook
Trained in the basements of Leeds during a three-year stint in the UK, Slowcook returned to Beijing with fire in her belly to match that of her record collection. Celebrated as a cult hero in Yorkshire for her ability to upstage the finest DJs across almost any genre, Slowcook became a part of the Zhao Dai establishment upon her return home, moving her patriarchy-disrupting Equaliser party with her. Having laid on workshops for women, non-binary and trans people in Leeds, Slowcook's vision of redressing imbalances in the music scene has been influential amidst the sudden proliferation of identity-affirmative partying in China, which now boasts a plethora of talented female DJs in particular.

Do Hits
Growing out of a party at Beijing's School Bar in 2011, Do Hits is an antidote to Western-centric Beijing clubbing institutions, championing a 'Made in China' approach driven by upcoming local producers including Howie Lee and Guzz. Under the stewardship of its early signings, Do Hits has grown into a multimedia collective and label, releasing VA compilations and tracks from Jason Hou, LOFIMAKER, Dokedo and more.

CLUB

Zhao Dai
Newcomer to the scene compared to the likes of Dada or Lantern, Zhao Dai has already set course to becoming a Beijing institution. One of the largest clubs in town, its sleek interior comes with possibly the best sound of any Chinese venue, in addition to mesmeric lighting and a raised dancing platform to give a little contour to the crowd. Having survived the pandemic by means of creative crowdfunding and the promised loyalty of its community, the Chaoyang district club has earned a reputation as a Petri dish of dance music culture; it embraces its audience with a headsy professionalism and an open-minded booking policy crafted by residents including co-owner Zhiqi, and Equaliser founder Slowcook.

CHENGDU

The centre of underground club culture in China, with the high rise .TAG club at its apex

Fondly referred to by many Chinese clubbers as 'Chengsterdam' for its comparatively European approach to underground culture, the provincial capital of Sichuan has become a popular pilgrimage site for China's growing dance music community, credited by those in the know as the most liberal (and liberating) party experience anywhere in the country. Whilst Shanghai and Beijing boast more clubs and longer underground histories, the business-first mindset that fuelled decades of economic growth feels omnipresent in both, and much harder to leave at the door of the club. Over in Chengdu, life is a few beats slower, and the politics a little more forgiving.

Make no mistake, though: with over 20 million people, Chengdu's residents are no strangers to the chaos of megacity living, nor the CCP's obsession with control. Nevertheless, in the perpetual sparring between underground art and state-imposed restrictions, leniency generally prevails more often in Chengdu than in other Chinese cities. The results of this are clear: nights last longer, people dance harder, and authorities' interferences are shorter and softer. "You feel like it's not inside of China at all", muses Beijing-based DJ Slowcook. "Chengdu is just heaven".

At the centre of this heaven, the legendary .TAG club hosts events that cross genres, push boundaries and show contempt for closing times,

encouraging floods of techno-tourists with its regular whole weekend parties. Most clubs are just clubs: spaces where dancing happens, blank canvases to be painted each night by their guests, and then brushed away like sand mandalas. Some, however, are something else entirely, rippling with an energy that seems to radiate well beyond its own walls. .TAG is one such place.

Those with time to explore might head east towards Funky Town, a tiny bar boasting a fiercely anti-establishment attitude, or spots like Cue Club and GUANXI along the same Kuhua Road. Avant-garde club AXIS lies north of the Jinjiang River, another staple venue in a scene that prides itself on subverting norms and preconceptions. Club hoppers should note that the Metro lines stop before 11pm, but taxis are cheap, so getting around during the silly hours won't be an issue.

With so much to explore in the murky underground, you could be forgiven for losing yourself to the night and neglecting the daytime in Chengdu, but in a city known for world-class food, a thriving art scene and a breathtaking combination of the historic and the futuristic throughout, that would be a mistake. A centre of innovation, yet also the only city in China to have retained its name for over two millennia, Chengdu's underground scene rests on cultural foundations that are centuries old.

The legendary .TAG club, at the centre of Chengdu's electronic music scene

Hao

Whilst it is Amsterdam that gives Chengdu its nickname, it's certainly Berlin that lends it its aesthetic, exemplified best by the city's most recognisable selector, Hao. Tall, tattooed and regularly dressed (or undressed) for Berghain, Hao is something of a techno icon in the city, commanding a residency at .TAG and frequently popping up at clubs around the country with his revered Seafood Party. In a country where LGBTQ+ rights still face significant social and political opposition, the presence of queer parties like Seafood is an important symbol of resistance and self-expression. Fittingly, Hao's aggressive sets conjure up a sense of battle march drums and the coursing of adrenaline.

Cora

Ultimately, .TAG is a techno club at heart, so it makes sense that resident Cora is best known as a purveyor of gritty percussion and fast, pulsating synth lines. Moving between trance-infused pounders, skippy minimal grooves and wig-out electro, her sets embody the spirit of Chengdu with their wild approach to the dancefloor, twisting and turning deep into the night and often beyond. A star at home and with an increasingly large following outside of Asia, it's easy to see why Chengdu's dancers hold Cora in such high regard.

CLUB

.TAG

A meeting point for the wild and bright-eyed, the imposing club sits at the top of a skyscraper, offering sunrise views as kick drums charge long into the morning. Acting almost as a La Masia for China's DJ community, it's a haven for those who treat clubbing not so much as a pastime but as a family ritual, and has given birth to much of China's new wave of electronic music devotees. With an ethos developed through the studious excursions of its founders to the world's best clubs, it is a party space designed for people to be people, in whatever shape and form they choose. "At . TAG, you don't go home until the sun rises", owner Ellen Zhang states with conviction. A leader from the front and the architect of the rich party scene, Zhang's vibrant personality is a good indication of why her club is widely regarded as the largest X on China's electronic music map.

TAIPEI

One of the few countries in Asia where gay marriage is legal, Taipei has a strong LGBTQ+ club scene

Unassuming, underrated and hugely underrepresented, Taipei might be Asia's best-kept clubbing secret

Whatever your flavour, whether it be big clubs and bottles (which it executes extremely well), or dark corners of dark rooms that are literally underground, a weekend in Taipei never lasts just one night. Credit to Luxy, a club that for more than 10 years was known and loved around Asia for its impassioned attempt at closing the gap between the over and underground across its sprawling three-room central Taipei location. The club's founders were responsible for bringing some of the biggest names in electronic music to the island, from Dr. Dre and Snoop Dogg to Tiësto and Paul Oakenfold, and you'd be hard-pressed to talk to someone who's been to Taipei and hasn't left with an amazing memory from the club.

But it's the underground music scene that really sets Taipei apart from other cities in Asia. While neighbouring countries throw big bucks for big names like Peggy Gou and Solomun, Taipei prefers a more leftfield sound palette and can fill a room with a single booking from Giegling or Ostgut Ton. Drawing influence from Japan in feeling and Berlin in sound, promoters in Taipei have done an excellent job in cultivating a largely Taiwanese music community who prefer off-kilter acts in a music scene that is largely free from foreigners (which is not the case in many cities across Asia that have expat-dominated dancefloors).

This is largely because of seminal club Korner, which opened in 2012 and closed in 2019. There were house and techno clubs before this, and Taipei was a regular stop for DJs like Sasha and Richie Hawtin in the 2000s, but it was Korner that nurtured a truly underground experience and gave an open, anything-goes platform for promoters to come in and do whatever they wanted. Taiwan-based and Berlin-bound label Smoke Machine percolated in Korner, and, at its peak, 1,000 kids dressed in black would come to the label's parties there to do the techno nod on the dancefloor for a night.

Korner is also where Bass Kitchen got its start, leaning towards the sunnier side of electronic music with its house-driven agenda. "I've been playing Bass Kitchen parties since 2013 and made friends for life in Taiwan because of them," says Move D. "The first party I ever played was in a former bottle cap factory with very authentic Berlin-style industrial wasteland vibes –a unique memory that will never fade. Now I even travel as far as Kaohsiung when I go to Taiwan. I'm a big fan of the Taiwanese people, culture and their little-but-dedicated electronic music scene."

Pawnshop rose from the ashes left behind by Korner. Already revered around the world, it is the first stop for a lot of DJs in Taiwan. Clubs like FINAL and Studio 9 are also new kids on the block;operated by scene stalwarts from venues like Korner and house and techno club B1 (which opened in 2018 in a converted underground parking garage), they are confidently here to stay. Taiwan's clubs have gotten so used to not overbooking international acts that venues have an incredibly sustainable model of operating without them. That said, its local DJs are still hugely underrepresented in the West, with the exception of Sonia Calico. So don't be disappointed if you go to Taiwan and are not familiar with the names on a line-up – trust the night to take you where you're meant to go. The magic of Taipei continues in its accessibility and affordability. Beneath its bathroom-tiled facades, you'll uncover a bustling and creative city with a well-refined music scene and even better post-clubbing food game (from restorative bubble tea to a breakfast of oyster vermicelli).

DJS / LABELS

Sonia Calcio
Sonia Calico weaves elements of Mandopop, instrumentation from traditional ceremonies and Japanese anime soundtracks into her soundscapes. But she also has a lofty vision, seeking to raise awareness of contemporary social issues through her releases, such as the marriage equality rights movement in Taiwan, and exploring themes around civilisation and future technologies. A recent landmark was curating the inaugural Synergy Festival in March 2022, similar to Sonar in its intersection of music and technology.

Diskonnected
SMOKE MACHINE's one and only resident, and one of Taipei's best exports. Diskonnected is one half of the driving force behind the label and its podcast series. For years, he appeared on nearly every line-up in Taiwan before taking off on a global tour in 2019, which saw him land in Los Angeles, Tel Aviv, London and a dozen more cities. Tastemaker and curator extraordinaire, don't forget to follow this extremely active DJ on SoundCloud until you can make it to Taiwan yourself.

SMOKE MACHINE
This enigmatic label has a cult-like following in Taipei and is well respected abroad. Perhaps most impressive since launching in 2019 is their SoundCloud account which is home to more than 220 mixes by artists like Rødhåd, Nobu, Kobosil, Ø [Phase], Gunnar Haslam, Etapp Kyle, Eric Cloutier, Vril, Ulf Eriksson, Mama Snake, Dr. Rubinstein, and more (many of whom played in Taiwan). Fun fact: SMOKE MACHINE'S founders also moonlight as the organisers of Organik.

禁 JIN
Founded by Yoshi Nori from one of Taiwan's oldest running music and nightlife brands Bass Kitchen, this label introduces Taipei-based talents to the world by pairing them with the right global minds, like linking French expat Romain FX with Bergen producer Telephones. The output is a sonic styling that morphs various elements into unpredictable forms of futuristic 4/4 sounds, foreshadowing the direction Asia's music scene is heading in.

CLUB / EVENT

Pawnshop
The second coming of the now-defunct Korner, Pawnshop is committed to brewing the next generation of talents and giving a platform to those who have an alternative vision of life. Despite opening just before the pandemic, the venue is continuously lauded by media outlets across the world as if it's been around for a decade (it kinda has). For now, Pawnshop is the first stop for techno junkies in Taiwan.

Organik
For a festival that only launched in 2014 and is still relatively unheard of, Organik consistently makes 'best festival' lists around the world. Perhaps it's due to its location, nestled along a black sand beach in Hualien on the eastern coast of Taiwan; perhaps it's due to its commitment to a small capacity, ensuring that its integrity and reputation are upheld; or perhaps it's the line-up, which is part-Berlin and part-Taiwan. Whatever the reason, it's well worthy of the trek.

SEOUL

In Korea's capital, Soju shots are the key to clubbers losing their inhibitions in the quasi-legal venues of Itaewon and Hongdae

Seoul's nightlife is shaped by the city's archaic licensing rules (drawn up for a pre/post-war nightlife economy built on semi-legal prostitution), and the city's high rents. Strictly speaking, clubs require a top tier alcohol licence – allowing dancing, lights and hostesses with drinks – and are heavily taxed, and most of these are concentrated in the Gangnam district. This is the centre of nightlife in the city, a neighbourhood of skyscrapers, 500+ capacity venues, hypercommercial EDM, champagne girls in bikinis, VIP tables and bottle service, concierge style service, and conspicuous consumption. Singing and outpourings of maudlin masculinity are more common than dancing in Gangnam, and the aftershocks of the Burning Sun club scandal still resonate, where a director of the club (also a member of one of Korea's biggest boy bands with political connections) was jailed after allegations of sexual assault, bribery and unlawful filming in the venue.

Thankfully, the neighbourhood of Itaewon has much more style. This is a compact district (its length can be walked across in about 10 minutes), but it's the centre of the underground scene and Seoul's LGBTQ+ community. Packed with great bars and an international, cosmopolitan vibe, its clubs compete to outdo each other in terms of their underground sensibility, some venues staying open seven days a week. Clubs here are necessarily small scale, operating in a quasi-legal situation where – in the absence of other revenue streams aside from cover charges and drinks – a restaurant licence, with its lower tax burden, is the only real option. This means venues have a limited capacity and are pretty discreet. Here's where you'll find industrial, stripped back spots like Volnost, RING and Concrete Bar offering house and techno with quality sound, deeply committed residents, local DJs like Conan and Xanexx, and the occasional overseas guest like Martyn or Thomas Von Party.

Ring, an industrial style venue at the heart of Seoul's techno scene

The third neighbourhood is Hongdae. This is where club culture arrived in Korea in the late 1990s, as the trance wave crested the planet. Less cut-throat than Itaewon when it comes to club competition, the scene is still led by some of those original adopters. MODECi and vurt. are two of the more interesting venues.

Seoul has two major raves: Air House, a party in the wilderness 40-minutes drive from the city, and High-Tech Seoul, which brings overseas techno stars to a warehouse across Yongsan Park from Itaewon. Both attract around 1,000+ people. Drugs are rare in Korean clubland, with LSD – untraceable, easy to smuggle – perhaps the most popular. Alcohol, however, is big – especially the local Soju spirit, distilled from potatoes. The locals stick it away in quantities comparable to the Celtic nations of Europe, fuelling an inhibitions-free culture of dancing, but the custom of having a shot when meeting every friend on a night out can quickly spiral. Then again, food is a crucial part of nights out in Seoul too, from meals beforehand with friends (accompanied by Soju, naturally) to a full post-club meal with the typically Korean proliferation of side dishes. Neighbourhoods like Itaewon and Gangnam have restaurants open 24 hours for when you need that kimchi infusion.

DJS

DJ Sin
A resident and music/creative director at Itaewon's Volnost club, Sin has been DJing since 2006, and set up the country's first female DJ crew, Triple House, with Suna and Mario. For three years they ran DIY parties in Seoul, taking care of everything from the decor to the music. Massively influenced by the Chicago sound of Derrick Carter, her sets range across house and techno.

Messiahwaits
Messiahwaits is considered Korea's brightest techno talent, with DJ bookings from Berlin to Los Angeles starting to reflect a growing global profile. A prolific techno producer, his releases have featured on compilations spanning Switzerland's queer techno collective Harder Traxxx to Tbilisi's INNERGATE (as well as releasing through his own MHz label).

CLUB / EVENT

RING
With its strict door policy, a ban on phones inside, and a vinyl-only requirement for DJs, RING might sound a little overzealous when it comes to keeping it real. But this emphatically industrial style venue is among the city's best in terms of atmosphere and music, despite only being open since 2020.

High-Tech Seoul
An occasional warehouse party that sees the clubs in Itaewon go quiet for a night as much of the scene decamps to a railway storage yard by Yongsan station, High-Tech Seoul is on a mission to bring international techno names like Amelie Lens, Dave Clarke and Rødhåd to the city, encourage local DJs, convert the curious and evangelise the city's enthusiasts.

○ RECORD SHOP

33
An invitation-only record shop and bar that specialises in acid, techno and house, 33 popped up during lockdown and reflects the still small but increasing demand for quality vinyl in the city. Still very much under the radar, find it by word of mouth.

BALI

<u>Lotus eaters, moped riders and Potato Heads make Bali more than just a stopover</u>

A beachside party at La Brisa

An enclave of Hinduism about the size of Greater London, Bali is an island outpost of the vast (and almost totally) Islamic country of Indonesia. Thanks to its easy-going atmosphere and idyllic climate and surroundings, it has long attracted tourists, lotus eaters and long-term escapees from reality from nearby (relatively speaking) Australia and across the world. It's also recently become something of a frontier town of the digital economy, a mecca for so-called digital nomads: life coaches, beachside bitcoin entrepreneurs, OnlyFans performers, aspiring influencers, and tech startups.

Despite its reputation as a party paradise, almost everything in Bali happens in the daytime: unsurprisingly, many visitors are content to surf, laze and pop into beach clubs. There are plenty of these, but Savaya in Uluwatu (formerly Omnia) is the diamond among them.

The (diurnal) 'nightlife' is centred in Kuta, where big daytime clubs like the huge ShiShi pump out tech house and bottle service to a pretty undiscerning crowd, and sprawling local DJ collective PNNY seem to have a finger in every pie being cooked right now. Dig deeper, though, and there is a scene to discover. Over in Canggu, the music community is a little more centred around smaller clubs and crews. Venues like Vault are a go-to on Friday and Saturday nights, and collectives like the Rainforest Pavilion and DESØNER organise regular events. The stunning La Brisa Bali on Echo Beach, a beachside terraced venue with decking built from the reclaimed wood of 500 fishing boats, has played host to Boiler Room events from DJs like Gerd Janson as well as their regular Basement Love parties by Tiago Oudman.

Among all the beach clubs that pepper Batu Belig Beach in Seminyak, Desa Potato Head stands out. The carefully manicured 'creative village', sustainable beach club and hotel has become a prime layover spot for touring DJs on their way back and forth from Europe to Australia, a favourite with the likes of HAAi, Ben UFO, Peggy Gou and Disclosure.

Bali's comparatively tardy lockdown initially attracted big international DJs looking for the last remaining global spots to play and earn, but when travel restrictions kicked in, it opened many a local venue booker's eyes to the indigenous talent across Indonesia, particularly in hip-hop and trap. The cooler fringe tends to keep moving north west, which is where you'll stumble upon elusive temple parties, moving up the island as commercialism and tourism creeps after it. Locals keep an eye on *The Yak* and *Mixmag Asia* for music news, parties and events.

Getting around will most likely involve a moped, and while everyone falls off at some point, riding sober is obviously recommended. Drugs are very illegal and very underground, and the itinerant here-today-gone-tomorrow expat population generally likes to start cocktail hour early, adding to the frontier vibe.

DJS / LABEL

Dea Barandara
A galaxy class crate digger once hailed by Gilles Peterson as "the best DJ I've heard in 10 years", Jakarta-born Barandana plays all over the world (and the occasional local party) from his studio base in Bali. Legend has it, he was once invited to play a private set for Grace Jones in her hotel room. Truly international and – in terms of music – unclassifiable.

Dita
Potato Head resident Dita is one of Bali's fastest rising DJ stars. Her 2022 Boiler Room Bali set was an odyssey through disco, synthy '80s style house and feel good esoteric – from Eris Drew to the Japanese brass and piano funk of the Tokyo Ska Paradise Orchestra.

Pantai People
Marc Robert's disco and edits focused label has found acclaim with everyone from David Morales to Austin Ato. Look out for the *Echo Beach Edits* EP series and their logo on flyers for events around Bali.

CLUB

Desa Potato Head
A single-minded focus on becoming the DJ destination and scene-leading spot in Bali has seen Potato Head expand Ushuaïa-style, from party space to glitzy beach hotel (and launch capsule collections with Peggy Gou). But it's also meant the best line-ups, with DJs playing music that actually fits the vibe of the Island, as well as some truly stunning design and architecture throughout.

HEADSTREAM studio space and record store, part of Desa Potato Head Beach Club

225

SYD NEY

Life after the lockout laws of 2014–2020 has forced this city to be creative, fuelling a new generation of DIY collectives running parties in unlikely venues

"The Sydney dance music scene is so diverse, but you have to search a bit deeper to find it," says local DJ Mincy. The 'lockout' laws that enforced curfews on the streets of Sydney's Kings Cross area from 2014 to 2020 paved the way for a cull of nightclubs and venues, and accelerated the transformation of the city's main club drag into a gentrified residential area. It also had an effect on a generation of clubland entrepreneurs, who moved into everything from hospitality to the restaurant industry. But the culture here is resilient, and the scarcity of dedicated traditional venues has fuelled the rise of a new generation of DIY collectives running parties across the city's indoor and outdoor spaces – and labels chock-full of talented DJs and producers. Look out for the likes of SHED:, Cocorico, Construct, Honey Trap Sound System and Mincy's own Extra Spicy, among countless others. Basement venue Club 77, just outside Kings Cross, is a long-established favourite, with a 20-year (if interrupted) history. Residents tend to carry the weight on nights like Code and Something Else, but look out for big guests when the festivals roll into town. Oxford Art Factory is a live venue that's also home to the 'proper house music' of S.A.S.H.

In Sydney, New Year's Day has always outshone New Year's Eve – unsurprising at the height of Summer. Daytime partying has stepped into the breach at venues like the Greenwood, a huge bar complex of connected courtyards, and the ivy precinct, a multipurpose venue of restaurants, patio, terraces and indoor spaces that welcomes international acts from Maceo Plex to Carl Cox and is the home of the POOF DOOF Sydney's queer parties. The Lord Gladstone, a punky dive bar-cum-burger bar style venue in

Connie Mitchell performs at POOF DOOF Sydney

Chippendale, is a less glitzy daytime hangout – and a good spot to ask the locals about the under-the-radar warehouse parties that pop up in the Inner West. Newtown and Enmore are the buzzing neighbourhoods to check out, full of bars, restaurants and, naturally for Australia, breweries.

As in many cities, in summer, raving moves out of the clubs and into the fields. Top festival events include Laneway, the massive Field Day on New Year's Day, Harbourlife, and Listen Out in October, full of big international electronic and hip-hop acts (think Diplo alongside Doja Cat). On the more boutique side of the festival scene is Output, a campout held on Castle Mountain just outside the city featuring Aussie artists like Assembler Code and Luen, and Electric Gardens Festival. And if the exhaustive festival season in and around Sydney isn't enough, you could always pack up the 'ute' and head out to a 'bush doof' or wilderness festival organised by the likes of Strawberry Fields, one of Australia's greatest party traditions.

Field Day, Sydney's biggest New Year's Day event

Jimi the Kween performs at POOF DOOF's outdoor festival

Flight Facilities
Sydney DJ/production duo Hugo Gruzman and James Lyell made their name remixing the likes of Bag Raiders and The C90s before a request from Bang Gang Records to create an original track resulted in their classic 2010 debut single 'Crave You'. Since then, they've released two albums (most recently *Forever* in 2021) and also an ambitious series of 'Decade Mixes'.

HAAi
She may have been born in the remote mining town of Karratha in Western Australia, but Teneil Throssell's formative years were spent in Sydney, albeit as part of a psychedelic rock band. Though she truly discovered her flair for DJing and production after a move to London, she's still considered a local hero – and a huge headline draw – on her not infrequent forays back to the city.

Sweat It Out
Co-founded by pioneering radio DJ and key member of The Bang Gang Deejays, Ajax, aka Adrian Thomas (much missed since his death in 2013), Sweat It Out, alongside Modular Recordings, put Australian electronic music on the global map. Growing out of the collective's legendary sessions in the then much smaller and sweatier Club 77, the label released the likes of Yolanda Be Cool and Oh Snap! and later signed RÜFÜS DU SOL. It put out What So Not's first release, which included a fresh-faced Flume.

Flight Facilities, Sydney's home-grown DJ/production duo

○ CLUB / RECORD SHOP

The Record Store
Despite its deeply unimaginative name, this Surrey Hills vendor is one of the country's most acclaimed, and also the home to much of Sydney's dance music royalty, including the iconic Kato, never seen DJing without his lucky Sweat It Out 'Tune' towel.

CLUB/EVENT

POOF DOOF Sydney
The flagship Saturday night at the giant ivy precinct, POOF DOOF is a beast of a clubbing brand, replete with drag queens, Aussie electronic icons and huge international guests nestled amid a music policy of accessible house.

Field Day
Held on New Year's Day at The Domain, the slightly sci-fi sounding location that turns out to be one of Sydney's most idyllic parks, Field Day is the big one when it comes to festivals. 2019's line-up was typical of the eclectic yet carefully curated range of artists featured each year, ranging from AJ Tracey and Cardi B to Kölsch and Bonobo.

MEL
BOU
RNE

This multicultural and
nightlife-positive city down
under is a festival paradise

Melbourne benefits from a large population of students, creatives and artists that keep its club, and especially its festival scene, one of the most vibrant in the Southern Hemisphere. Such is the appetite for electronic music that a 'niche' underground DJ, touring or local, can fill a 300-cap club here with ease. 24-hour licences are rare and passed down through generations of owners (the authorities have stopped issuing them, so when a venue closes its doors they are gone forever), so nightlife starts late here and clubs are open until 5am.

One of those licences is still held, however, by the famous Revolver Upstairs. More than 25 years strong, it is still open from Thursday night non-stop until Sunday, with residents and international guests of the calibre of Ben UFO, Gerd Janson, FJAAK and DJ Boring. Unlike Revolver, most of the key clubs are found close to each other in the CBD or Central Business District. Here you'll find the likes of new techno venue Sub Club, the 1,200 capacity Brown Alley, and Xe54, with its focus on emerging electronic artists and DJs from across the world. Most pre-clubbing is done at house parties before heading out at midnight, but there are buzzing bar neighbourhoods, such as Prarhan (where Revolver is based) and Brunswick South, to while away the hours before then.

O RECORD SHOP

Licorice Pie Records
There are so many great record shops in Melbourne that each year local vinyl lovers create a tour guide – get the latest map from digginmelbourne.com. Licorice Pie is one store notable for its huge (10,000 strong) vinyl collection, full of unexpected gems and rarities across genres from disco and boogie to jazz and avant-garde.

Besides the clubs, the festival and one-off event scene booms in Melbourne and the surrounding area. From boutique, single stage events like Inner Varnika, held two hours west of the city with an all-Victorian (the state not the era) line-up of artists, to the massive, all-star Pitch Music & Arts festival; from parties at open-air sites within the city limits like Abbots Yard or the Coburg Velodrome to those held in converted warehouses such as the 5,000 capacity Wool Store (where you might find the likes of Patrick Topping or Jamie Jones shearing the sound system), there are dozens of events all year round and particularly throughout the Aussie summer. And if your tastes run to the more intimate, look out for little bars like Miscellania, Section 8 and Hope St Radio, all pushing great music every weekend.

Public transport – trams and trains – runs all night in Melbourne, and, licences aside, the authorities are generally supportive of the scene. Initiatives like White Night (an annual light festival held in February, which celebrates the nighttime economy by lighting up the CBD) and cultural grants and permits for events on greenfield sites keep the scene healthy and relevant.

Ben UFO and Moopie DJing at Sub Club Melbourne

DJ Jnett

A stalwart of the scene since the '90s, Janette Pitruzzello is DJ royalty in Melbourne. A former record picker for the city's famed Central Station record store who's also presented club themed shows on TV and radio, Jnett's sets span disco, deep house, reggae and even hip-hop, while as a producer she's released on Maurice Fulton's BubbleTease label.

Boogs

Enigmatic Revolver resident DJ Boogs has a cult following across the city thanks to his Sunday morning sessions at the club, a riot of house, techno and tech house which have been running, incredibly, since 2001. You can also catch him at events like Thick as Thieves, a long-running collective holding parties across the city with a focus on underground Aussie stars.

Modular Recordings

Sydney might have slightly more of a claim on Modular, but there's no doubt that Melbourne artists like The Avalanches and Cut Copy were a huge part of the golden age of Australian electronic music that the label powered in the late '00s. By connecting the scenes of the two cities and releasing a string of classic singles and albums that defined a new sound for the country, Modular had a worldwide impact.

Sub Club Melbourne

Aiming to blur the lines between club venue and art project, Sub Club is a recently opened intimate space that's positioned itself to champion breakthrough and new artists from the local and international scene, from the raw industrial techno of Melbourne's Mickey Knox and DJ ALI to Afrofuturist live duo The Illustrious Blacks.

Pitch Music & Arts

This 7,500-capacity four-day camping festival held over 230km away from the city on the volcanic Grampian plains is still considered a Melbourne Festival (this is Australia after all). The 2022 line-up featured more than 30 international DJs, from Sherelle to Maceo Plex to Floating Points, spanning house, techno, disco and more. Offshoot Pitch Black hosts events in the city with the likes of DJ Seinfeld and CC:DISCO!.

ABOUT THE AUTHOR

Appointed Mixmag magazine Editor in 2015, Duncan Dick was born in the small village of Killearn just outside Glasgow and is currently based in Brixton, London. The editor of *The Secret DJ: Tales From The Booth* (2021) and *The Secret DJ Book II* (2019), he is also the author of a book on Copenhagen's Coma Club. A very occasional DJ with a definite weakness for disco edits of Fleetwood Mac, and an evangelist for the power of club culture as a force for equality, community and creativity, he founded content studio Devil's Ivy Creative in 2021.

ACKNOWLEDGEMENTS

The author would like to thank

Pete Jorgensen at DK / Penguin Random House, editor Florence Ward and proofreader Madeleine Pollard.

Nick Stevenson, the team at Mixmag / Mixmag.net and all contributors past and present, as well as the writers behind the many other great resources – from long read features to humble club listings – that have helped me fill in the gaps.

Tracy Kawalik, Shirley Ahura, Olivia Wycech, Andrew Kemp, Nicolas Dembicki, Fede Rochon, Nicolas Gonzalez, Ivi Brasil and Eduardo Oliviera.

Ralph Moore, Patrick Hinton and Vassilis Skandalis for the extra pairs of eyes.

The locals:

Alice Austin

Kat Bein

Ciel

Nick Clarke

Inês Borges Coutinho

Marie-Charlotte Dapoigny

Nick DeCosemo

Marouane Ferchichi

Koen Galle

Belen Gandolfo

IAJ

Hayley Illing

Quincy Kim

David McGraw

Monty McGaw

Miroslav Miletic

Czarina Mirani

Lily Moayeri

David Muallem

Jack Murphy

David Pollock

Arun Ramathan

Joe Roberts

Marc Roberts

Kamila Rymajdo

Seni Saraki

Reisa Shanaman

Sunil Sharpe

Tiga Sontag

Stefon

Paul Stix

Thom Svast

The Secret DJ

Ivan Turanjanin

Ryan Vermaak

Artur Wojtczak

All the promoters, venue owners, artists, stream teams, DJs, and most of all the clubbers, who keep this global culture alive and evolving.

238

Additional reporting:
46-49 (Toronto): with Tracy Kawalik. 56-59 (Mexico City): with Tracy Kawalik. 60-61 (Rio de Janeiro): additional reporting from Ivi Brasil and Eduardo Oliveira. 62-65 (São Paulo): additional reporting from Ivi Brasil and Eduardo Oliveira. 66-67 (Santa Catarina): additional reporting from Ivi Brasil and Eduardo Oliveira. 68-71 (Buenos Aires): additional reporting from Nicolas Dembicki. 72-73 (Montevideo): additional reporting from Fede Rochon. 74-79 (Santiago): with Nicolas Gonzalez. 140-141 (Rotterdam): with Holly Dicker. 182-185 (Kampala): with Shirley Ahura. 214-215 (Bangkok): with Olivia Wycech. 216-217 (Beijing): with Andrew Kemp. 218-219 (Chengdu): with Andrew Kemp. 220-221 (Taipei): with Olivia Wycech

Pictures:
The publisher would like to thank the following for their kind permission to reproduce their photographs:

(Key: a-above; b-below/bottom; c-centre; f-far; l-left; r-right; t-top)

2-3: ShotAway for Junction 2 Festival. **9:** Ian Hindmarsh, with thanks to Alon Shulman at World Famous Group. **10-11:** Med Mhamdi. **14:** Ellina Martsynenko. **16:** Ellina Martsynenko. **17:** Music by Marina. **18-19:** Guillaume Chottin. **21:** Image courtesy of Smartbar. **22-23:** Alamy Stock Photo: Jim Newberry. **24:** Kristin Adamczyk. **26:** Kristin Adamczyk (tl); Rui Soares (bl). **27:** Kristin Adamczyk. **28-29:** Anthony Rassam for Movement Festival. **30-31:** Kristin Adamczyk. **33:** Lauren DeCanio for Unreal. **34-35:** @adiadinayev for Infamous. **36-37:** Christian Villarreal for Unreal. **39:** Jesse Hudson (bl); Getty Images: NurPhoto (tr). **40-41:** Alamy Stock Photo: WENN Rights Ltd. **43:** Alamy Stock Photo: MediaPunch Inc (tr); Ally Connolly / Stockimo (br). **44:** Rob Jones for Love International. **48:** Danny Voicu. **49:** Danny Voicu. **50:** Soft Melancholy. **51:** Alamy Stock Photo: ZUMA Press, Inc. **52-53:** M Belmellat for Nuits D'Afrique. **58:** Alejandro Misteró. **59:** Alejandro Misteró (a); Alejandro Misteró (b). **61:** Diego Padilha. **63:** Nicolas Gonzalez. **64-65:** Nicolas Gonzalez. **66:** Ebraim Martini. **68:** destinoarena. **70-71:** Isaías Bovio for destinoarena. **73:** Jake Davis for Love International. **74-75:** Nicolas Gonzalez. **76:** Nicolas Gonzalez. **77:** Nicolas Gonzalez. **78-79:** Nicolas Gonzalez. **83:** Jake Davis. **84:** Music by Marina (tl); Alamy Stock Photo: Georgina Cook / Everynight Images (bl). **85:** Luke Dyson for Junction 2 Festival. **86-87:** Getty Images: Carl Court. **89:**

Jody Hartley. **90-91:** Rob Jones. **92:** Rob Jones (tl); Rob Jones (bl). **93:** Rob Jones (tr); Rob Jones (tr). **94-95:** Alamy Stock Photo: Trinity Mirror / Mirrorpix. **96:** Kierian Patton. **98:** Kierian Patton. **99:** Michael Hunter. **100-101:** Jake Davis for Love International. **103:** Daniel Rrell. **104:** EMA (l). **105:** Sunil Sharpe. **107:** Subtyl. **108:** Music by Marina. **109:** Alamy Stock Photo: Marcin Rogozinski. **110-111:** Music by Marina. **112-113:** Alamy Stock Photo: Niall Carson / PA Images. **115:** Kevin Lake. **116:** Pablo Bustos. **118-119:** Kevin Lake. **121:** Astrid Bosch and Nicolas Clausen. **122-123:** Pablo Bustos. **125:** Rui Soares. **126:** Rui Soares. **127:** Rui Soares. **129:** Veronica Bottan. **130:** Alamy Stock Photo: david pearson (t); Gabriele Canfora (Lagarty Photo) for Amnesia Milano (b). **131:** Marco Walker for Measure. **132-133:** Alamy Stock Photo: Sipa US. **135:** Jeremy Gérard. **137:** Aileen de Ruijter. **138-139:** Alamy Stock Photo: Scott Mcquaide / EyeEm. **141:** Dreamstime.com: Frans Blok. **142:** Alamy Stock Photo: Kay Nietfeld / dpa picture alliance. **144-145:** Pablo Bustos (a). **145:** Pablo Bustos (b). **146-147:** Alamy Stock Photo: dpa picture alliance. **149:** Getty Images: Martyn Goodacre / Hulton Archive (tl); Simon Vorhammer (tr). **151:** Alamy Stock Photo: Juan Jimenez (t). **152:** Alamy Stock Photo: Flemming Bo Jensen / Gonzales Photo. **153:** Mantas Hesthaven. **154-155:** Image courtesy of Coma Club. **156:** Helena Majewska. **158-159:** Image courtesy of INSTYTUT. **161:** Milivoje Bozovic. **162-163:** Khris Cowley. **165:** Jake Davis for Love International. **166-167:** Pablo Bustos. **169:** George Nebieridze. **170:** Pablo Bustos. **171:** George Nebieridze. **172-173:** George Nebieridze. **177:** Med Mhamdi. **178-179:** Joe Plimmer. **180:** Joe Plimmer. **181:** Joe Plimmer. **184-185:** Bwette photography. **187:** Image courtesy of Mødular. **189:** Music by Marina. **190:** Joffrey Hyman. **191:** Ryan Vermaak (tr); Kgothatso Meko (br). **193:** BOJ Studios. **196:** Ben Palhov. **197:** Ben Palhov. **200:** Ron Bezbaruah. **202:** Alamy Stock Photo: Rakesh Dhareshwar. **203:** Rajvi Vaya. **204-205:** Image courtesy of I Love Goa (facebook.com/ilovegoaparties). **207:** Mark Oxley. **208:** Mark Oxley. **209:** Mark Oxley. **210:** Mark Oxley. **211:** Mark Oxley. **212-213:** Cedric Bardawil. **215:** Image courtesy of Wonderfruit. **216:** Zhang Ranyue. **219:** Tao Yun. **220:** Gregory Garde. **223:** Hansy. **224:** Image courtesy of La Brisa. **225:** Image courtesy of Potato Head. **227:** Pat Stevenson. **228:** Anna Warr for Field Day (a); Pat Stevenson (b). **229:** Alamy Stock Photo: Richard Milnes. **231:** William Hamilton-Coates. **237:** Joe Plimmer.

Cover image: Sam Neill

Penguin
Random
House

Editor Florence Ward

Senior Designer Lauren Adams

Senior Production Editor Jennifer Murray

Senior Production Controller Louise Minihane

Senior Acquisitions Editor Pete Jorgensen

Managing Art Editor Jo Connor

Publishing Director Mark Searle

Text Duncan Dick

With additional text by Shirley Ahura, Ivi Brasil, Nicolas Dembicki, Holly Dicker, Nicolas Gonzalez, Tracy Kawalik, Andrew Kemp, Eduardo Oliviera, Fede Rochon and Olivia Wycech

Design concept Eoghan O'Brien

Layouts designed for DK by Lisa Lanzarini

DK would like to thank Madeleine Pollard for proofreading and Helen Peters for indexing.

First American Edition, 2022
Published in the United States by DK Publishing
1745 Broadway, 20th Floor, New York, NY 10019

Page design copyright © 2022 Dorling Kindersley Limited
DK, a Division of Penguin Random House LLC
22 23 24 25 26 10 9 8 7 6 5 4 3 2 1
001–332742/–Nov/2022

Text copyright © 2022 Duncan Dick

A catalog record for this book is available from the Library of Congress.
ISBN: 978-0-7440-6393-4

DK books are available at special discounts when purchased in bulk for sales promotions, premiums, fund-raising, or educational use. For details, contact:
DK Publishing Special Markets, 1745 Broadway, 20th Floor, New York, NY 10019
SpecialSales@dk.com

Printed and bound in Slovakia
For the curious
www.dk.com

MIX
Paper | Supporting
responsible forestry
FSC™ C018179

This book was made with Forest Stewardship Council ™ certified paper—one small step in DK's commitment to a sustainable future. For more information go to www.dk.com/our-green-pledge.